This Kind of Love

This Kind of Love

The Overwhelming Power of
PROMISES, PATIENCE, and FAITH

KAELIN *and* KYRAH
EDWARDS

New York • Nashville

Worthy
Hachette Book Group
1290 Avenue of the Americas, New York, NY 10104
worthypublishing.com
twitter.com/worthypub

First Edition: July 2021

Worthy Publishing is a division of Hachette Book Group, Inc. The Worthy Publishing name and logo are trademarks of Hachette Book Group, Inc.

The publisher is not responsible for websites (or their content) that are not owned by the publisher.

The Hachette Speakers Bureau provides a wide range of authors for speaking events. To find out more, go to www.hachettespeakersbureau.com or call (866) 376-6591.

All Scripture quotations taken from The Holy Bible, English Standard Version. ESV® Text Edition: 2016. Copyright © 2001 by Crossway Bibles, a publishing ministry of Good News Publishers.

Library of Congress Cataloging-in-Publication Data
Names: Edwards, Kaelin, author. | Edwards, Kyrah, author.
Title: This kind of love : the overwhelming power of promises, patience, and faith / Kaelin Edwards and Kyrah Edwards.
Description: First edition. | New York : Worthy, 2021. | Summary: "Kaelin and Kyrah Edward's viral video of 2016 (Crazy Girlfriend Throws iPhone in the Pool!) thrust them into the spotlight with a velocity that they never could have imagined. Since that time, they have grown up in front of their audience - they have built their relationship, gotten married, grown their family through the births of their two little boys. What began for them as the posting of a prank video has evolved into an engaged viewership of over 2 million on their various social channels that looks to them for guidance in how to make good life decisions. This Kind of Love follows the Edwards' family's adventure as they learn to live through the lens of God's promises and principles, such as: Waiting to have sex until marriage out of obedience to God's plan for our lives. Waiting to take the time to lay a foundation for our future rather than rushing to get on with life. Waiting for God's plan for our lives to be revealed. Waiting for God's timing. Waiting for God to refine our character. Waiting for one another to become who we will be. Waiting for God to come through when trouble comes. In This Kind of Love, Kaelin and Kyrah invite you to join their often tumultuous journey and experience—alongside of them—the joy and beauty that comes through waiting for God to do His work in our lives"—Provided by publisher.
Identifiers: LCCN 2021006602 | ISBN 9781546017523 (hardcover) | ISBN 9781546017530 (ebook)
Subjects: LCSH: Marriage—Religious aspects—Christianity. | Families—Religious aspects—
    °Christianity. | Edwards family.
Classification: LCC BV835 .E39 2021 | DDC 248.4--dc23
LC record available at https://lccn.loc.gov/2021006602

Printed in Canada

MRQ-T

10 9 8 7 6 5 4 3 2 1

To our parents, whose shoulders we stand on.
There is no us without you.

Contents

PROLOGUE

Over the past four years, we've opened our lives to you via YouTube through our channel, *Kaelin and Kyrah*. You've walked with us as we've grown from a couple of teenagers getting married to the parents of two young sons living fifteen hundred miles away from all our friends and family in the midst of a global pandemic. Many of you have laughed with us and cried with us and worried with us. We've rejoiced and experienced all the ups and downs life has thrown at us. Through it all, we've grown, in every direction, together. That's what makes us more than just a "community." The two of us feel like you've become members of our family.

Around the time we did our first "storytime" video, we started talking about writing a book. Back then, we thought we'd write about how we met and fell in love, all leading up to our dream wedding. We planned to weave our Christian faith into this narrative, especially emphasizing how we waited to have sex until marriage. We planned to call the book *Worth the Wait*, which seemed like the perfect fit at the time. The book would build up to the moment we said, "I do," and close with us headed off into our happily ever after.

A funny thing happened on our way to writing that book, and that funny thing is called life. Six months after we were married, we found out Kyrah was pregnant. The birth of our son Karter changed us more than we'd ever thought possible. We were forced to grow up fast after becoming parents. Adding a newborn to the other challenges we faced as a young Christian couple trying to figure out our place in this world—I'm surprised we kept it all together. There's no manual for dealing with the challenges and responsibilities of adulthood. That's why, when our second son, Kaiser, came along just over a year later, the two of us knew we were no longer the people who had planned to write a fairy-tale romance. We also knew you wanted more than that from us. You deserved the unfiltered truth. Our "happily ever after" was not the climax of our story, but the beginning. What we have learned about each other and ourselves since we said, "I do," has completely transformed us, and continues to do so day after day.

And that's the journey we once again invite you to take with us through the pages of this book. We will take you deeper than we ever could online as you learn the inside story of both the struggles and the victories we never felt completely comfortable sharing on YouTube. The story you are about to read isn't always pretty, but that's the beauty of it. Life never goes the way we expect. We've learned that the more life has gone off script, the more we have had to rely upon God, who is always at work. This story you are about to read is also unfinished because our little family is still a work in progress. As you read the journey we've taken together thus far, please know that we can't wait to see where God will take us next. Looking back, it's hard to believe that it all started outside a portable classroom at Earl Warren Junior High School in Bakersfield, California.

This Kind of Love

Junior High Romance

KAELIN:

Back in sixth grade, I played on a little league football team in my hometown of Bakersfield, California. A couple of the guys on the team, Keon and Jaylan, went to a different school. And all they ever talked about was the girls they liked at their school. One person they couldn't stop mentioning was this girl named Kyrah. Anytime I got close to them, all I heard was Kyrah this and Kyrah that. Every once in a while, Jaylan or Keon would mention her friend Arianna, but most of the time it was just Kyrah, Kyrah, Kyrah. Now, I had my own girls in my school I had my eye on, so I didn't think too much about trying to find out more about theirs. However, the more they talked about this girl Kyrah, the more I started to wonder what it was that made her so special.

Fast-forward one year to the first day of junior high. Keon and I ended up in the same school. Not only that, we compared schedules and we had the same English class. The problem was, neither one of us could find it. We were tripping through the halls, looking for this impossible-to-find classroom. It turns out it wasn't even a real classroom but a portable at the back of the school grounds. Apparently, our school was at capacity, so they brought portables in over the summer to make room for everyone. Once we finally figured out where we needed to go, we headed toward the portables. Keon and I were halfway across the blacktop when I saw this girl standing on the ramp leading up to the classroom we were looking for. I could not take my eyes off her. I punched my friend Keon and asked him, "Whoa, bro, who is that?"

"That's Kyrah," Keon said.

"*That's* Kyrah!?" I said. "That's the girl y'all couldn't shut up about last year?"

"Yeah, man. That's Kyrah."

"Okay…Now I get it. Keon, bro, you know you have to introduce me to her, right?"

Keon gave me a look like, *Why would I ever do that? I ain't crazy.*

"You don't like her, do you?" I teased.

"No, man, that's Jaylan's girl. We're just friends," he shot back.

"Well, Jaylan doesn't go here," I said with a shrug, "and besides, I just want to be her friend too."

We approached the ramp. The bell was about to ring. I didn't have much time. Kyrah was talking to someone and didn't pay any attention to Keon and me. My mind was racing, thinking of some way to break the ice in case Keon flaked on me. All at once, the girl Kyrah was talking with noticed Keon and shouted his name.

"Keon!" she yelled.

"Arianna!" he yelled back. He walked up to her and gave her a hug.

I could tell Arianna and Keon were relieved to see each other.

"Hey, Kyrah," Keon said as he gave her a side hug.

I couldn't wait for Keon to introduce me. "I'm Kaelin," I said as I stuck out my hand. "Keon and I play football together and have been friends for years. It's nice to meet you both."

"Hi, Kaelin, it's nice to meet you," Arianna and Kyrah said at the same time, although Kyrah spoke more softly than Arianna.

They must be pretty close to answer together like that, I thought, *and Kyrah must be pretty shy. That's cute.*

The bell rang before I could say anything else, but I wasn't worried. I'd get my chance. We were already in the same first-period English class and fourth-period literature. Since fourth period was our homeroom for the year, not only would I see her at least twice a day, but we'd also be in the same group for drills, assemblies, trips, and other school events as well. Now all I had to do was sit near her, find an excuse to talk to her, and away we'd go. The teacher, however, didn't exactly make my plan easy. When we got into class, she had us all stand around against the wall until she assigned our seats to us. That's when I noticed my best friend Brandon was also in this class. Now Keon, Brandon, and I were three of the handful of Black guys in this school, and all three of us were now in the same English class with Kyrah…I knew the race was about to be on as to who could get to her first. I'm a pretty competitive guy. The winner in the race for Kyrah's affection needed to be me.

The teacher assigned seats, and as if God ordained it, I ended up right next to Kyrah!

I only wish that were true. No, the teacher put me on the complete opposite side of the room. It was like she knew my plans and was telling me, *Don't you even think about trying to get close to this girl.* Thankfully, neither Keon nor Brandon was anywhere close to Kyrah either, which was good for me. I did a quick study of the room and started making plans to get to know one of the girls near Kyrah and then talk her into trading seats with me. My plan might have worked except our class was too full and the school moved Brandon and me to a different first-period English class and fourth-period literature class the second day of school. I'm sure Kyrah had to be as disappointed as I was.

KYRAH:

I had no idea who Kaelin Edwards was or even that he was in any of my classes the first day of seventh grade. When the teacher lined us up around the walls while she assigned us our seats, I wasn't checking out the cute boys. Well, maybe a little. Mostly I was looking around to see if I knew anyone other than Arianna and Keon. My parents moved from one side of Bakersfield to the other the summer between sixth and seventh grades. Nearly everyone with whom I went to grade school ended up at a different junior high. Arianna and Keon were basically the only people I knew. The three of us quickly became friends, even though we hadn't really been that close in elementary school.

I don't think I could have survived junior high without Arianna and Keon. I don't know how it is for guys, but for girls, junior high pretty much sucks—it did for me, at least. Having to make a whole new set of friends made it that much worse. The school was primarily white, and as one of the few mixed girls in my grade, I was too Black for most of the white girls and too white for the handful of Black girls. Maybe that's not how they saw me, but that's how I saw myself. I ended up finding a group of girls who became my friends, but the more I was with them, the more my life started to feel like the movie *Mean Girls*. At lunch I'd find them in the cafeteria, but I always ended up sitting on the outside of the group. They'd all whisper about something among themselves. "What?" I'd ask with a smile and a little laugh. "Oh, nothing," they'd say, if they answered me at all. They were just as likely to ignore me like I wasn't even there. A couple of them lived near me, so in order to be more social and make friends, I asked my mom and dad if I could walk home with them. After last period, I'd rush to the outside gates to wait for them to make sure they didn't leave without me. I'd wait for them to show up. And I'd wait. And I'd wait until I'd realize that they'd already left. After getting stood up, I'd trudge home. Alone. One time, as soon as I walked in the door, I burst into tears. When my mom asked what was wrong, I yelled, "No one likes me!"

"I think you're being a little dramatic," my mom replied.

KAELIN:

Kyrah obviously had no idea I was interested in her. Even after being moved out of her class, I could not stop thinking about her. I had to find a way to get to know her, but at that age no one just goes up and tells someone, "Hey, I like you. Do you like me?" No one, especially me, wanted to risk that kind of rejection. You could never live it down. No, I had to play it cool. I needed to come up with a plan to win her heart.

I watched Kyrah from afar and noticed that of all the people I saw her hanging around, she spent more time with Arianna than anyone else. *That's my opening*, I thought. Arianna had sat next to me when I'd been in her and Kyrah's English class, and fortunately I'd been smart enough to get her number the first day. It took a couple of weeks, but Arianna and I became pretty good friends. After building rapport with her, I asked her about her friend Kyrah one day. "I want to play a prank on her and text her really quick," I said, "but I don't have her number." I don't know if Arianna fully believed me, but she believed me enough to give me Kyrah's number. That's all I needed. Before long, Kyrah and I were texting back and forth every day.

Now here's where the story gets a little tricky for me. The more I talked to Kyrah, the more I liked her. I wanted to ask her out, which doesn't mean the same in seventh grade as it does in the real world. No one ever went *out* on any actual dates. Going out meant you hung out in the hallways between class and during lunch and before and after school. However, even the junior high version of going out made me take a step back because I knew that the moment my boys found out that I had a girlfriend, they'd be all up in my business and giving me a hard time. I also come from a large family. I am the youngest of six. The second my brothers and my sisters found out that I had a girlfriend, I would never hear the end of it—especially from my older sister, Kelsie. She's about four years older than me, but she had a history of telling on my siblings and me to my parents. Even worse, I had to make sure my older brother Kameron didn't find out. He is only two years older than me, and we shared the SAME friends. If my friends found out and made it a big deal, I knew it would only be a matter of time before word got to him.

However, since this was junior high, if you kept talking to the same girl or guy long enough, you were expected to ask them to be your boyfriend or girlfriend. And Kyrah expected me to ask her. But I never did. She started asking me why I wouldn't. I told her I needed more time. She went from asking me why I didn't to basically telling me I needed to ask her to be my girlfriend. I told her I would if we could keep it a secret. "Why would you want to keep this a secret?" she asked. When she put it that way, nothing seemed like a good answer. I could tell her that all my friends would give me a hard time about her or that my sisters would never let me hear the end of it, but I knew those excuses wouldn't fly. I wasn't embarrassed by her possibly being my girlfriend, but it sure did sound that way. I really did like her and wanted to be her boyfriend; it's just at that age you're not screaming who your crush is from the rooftops.

Finally, I asked her to be my junior high girlfriend. And she said yes. After that, the best part of my day was seeing her at lunch or giving her a hug goodbye in front of the school after the last bell rang. I hate orange, but I'd wear my only orange shirt every week since it was her favorite color back then. I promised her that I'd never break up with her. That was a big commitment for a seventh grader. I guess I was always kind of a hopeless romantic. Even though we tried to keep our relationship a secret, people saw us together and figured out what was really going on. As I expected, my friends all gave me a hard time about her, but I know they were just jealous. How could they not have been? She was the prettiest girl in school.

KYRAH:

I really liked Kaelin. Even though we were only in seventh grade, our conversation flowed seamlessly. We would text and talk on the phone nonstop. He really was my best friend. We didn't have any classes together, but we always stole a little time at the end of the day after the last bell rang to say goodbye. That was the best part of my day. Sitting in my last class, I'd look up at the clock, knowing the bell was about to ring, and butterflies would fill my stomach. I'd feel so nervous and excited, like this was the only part of my day that even mattered. And then I'd see him waiting for me. We'd talk, but we'd never get to talk long because most days one of my parents picked me up. If my dad happened to pull up to the school and saw me hugging a boy, he'd kill me. When Kaelin and I were together, my head constantly swept back and forth as I watched for my dad. At the same time, I did not want my few minutes with Kaelin to end. Nothing felt better than having him take me in his arms and hug me goodbye. We were young, but it was so sweet and so innocent and so wonderful.

KAELIN:

Two months later, Kyrah sent me a text and said that we should just be friends. We talked it through and we both agreed it was for the best. "I still like you, but…Maybe when we're older we can try it again," Kyrah said.

"I still like you too; maybe then people will stay out of our business," I said, but I don't know how serious either of us was about actually trying again. We were only twelve and it was hard to think that far into the future. To be honest, I was probably as ready to move on as she was, but I had to keep my promise not to break up with her. Regardless, having her bring up breaking up first hurt my ego. At least we'd made it two months.

Two months is a long time in junior high years. Even though we'd said we'd remain friends, I never talked to her when I saw her around school the rest of seventh grade and through eighth. It was just not the same. We also stopped texting. We went from a burning-hot junior high romance to practically strangers. Eventually I moved on to other girls, but I always wondered what could have been with us. *Would we really wait for each other?* Our junior high romance might have been over, but my crush on her lingered on.

KYRAH:

So why did I break up with Kaelin? I felt like I needed to. My dad had made it very, *very* clear to me that I was not to date any boy until I turned sixteen. No exceptions. Even though Kaelin and I weren't actually dating, since we were both a few years from being old enough to get a driver's license and actually go out, I didn't think my dad would buy that technicality. No dating until I was sixteen meant no boys until I turned sixteen. He was always very protective of me in that way. I had managed to keep my relationship with Kaelin a secret for as long as I thought possible. I felt it was just a matter of time before my dad found out.

My dad had a knack for finding out everything I did, even though his work with the railroad took him out of town for days at a time. He went onto my social media accounts and read everything I posted. Sometimes he'd come into my room at night, take my phone, and go through my texts and phone calls. Before you say you can't believe he'd do something like that, you have to remember that I was only twelve or thirteen years old and my dad was away a lot. He told me that when he went away for work, he had to put his all into his job. All of our livelihoods depended on him being able to concentrate fully on work without anyone taking him out of his comfort zone. He couldn't do his job while also worrying about me and my siblings. While I wish he would've had more trust in me, I understand, now that I'm a mom, that he was only trying to protect me. However, at the time, I lived in fear that he'd discover my secret romance and I'd be in big trouble.

I think that's part of the reason why I broke up with Kaelin. Honestly, I don't remember all that went into that decision. We were only in seventh grade, so it's not like I ever thought our love affair was going to last forever. Like I said earlier, junior high wasn't exactly the greatest time in my life. School was hard. Girls were mean. I felt like I never fit in. It makes me sad just thinking about it! I only hoped to survive and move on to high school.

School wasn't the only thing that made this such a hard time in my life. My parents never really got along, but I didn't start to notice until junior high. Maybe they did a better job of hiding it before then, or maybe I was just too young to realize what was going on. Whatever the reason, their fighting became a constant in our home. I'd never heard the word divorce mentioned before then, but now it got thrown around all the time.

As the fighting increased, so did my fear that a day was coming when my dad would be gone. I'll never forget the first time I saw his suitcases near the front door. He stood there, telling us that he was leaving. Before he could walk out the door, though, he started crying. "It's not supposed to be this way," he said. Then my mom started crying and I started crying and my little brother and two little sisters started crying. The suitcases ended up going back to my parents' room. "Things are going to be different," both my mom and dad announced later in a big family meeting. I think the first time this happened they told us that we weren't spending enough time together as a family, so from now on Sundays were going to be family days. I loved the sound of that. For a few weeks, our family became this perfect little white-picket-fence ideal of a family. But it didn't last. A month or so later, my parents were back at it, fighting like before. Then the suitcases came back out, followed by a change of heart and a promise that things were going to change. The change would last for a month; then the cycle would repeat itself.

I don't fault my parents. They were struggling to hold it all together with my dad gone all the time while my mom stayed home with us kids. Now that I'm a mom of two young boys, also juggling family with the demands of work, I know holding it all together isn't easy. However, I didn't have that insight back then. Watching my parents' marriage come apart in very, very slow motion wasn't easy for me. It's not for anyone living through that experience. Both of my parents have volatile tempers, something I inherited as well. Growing up, I never learned how to control my emotions. When I started crying, I cried so hard I hyperventilated and could not breathe. When I became angry in my adult years, I would get so mad I wouldn't be able to control the rage inside of me. Any time I became upset, my mother always took my side. Nothing was ever my fault. If a teacher got onto me, my mom would call the school to confront them. If I had a problem with a friend on the playground, my mom would always blame the friend, not me. Only after getting married did I see how fully I had embraced victimhood and how destructive it can be on a relationship. Junior high me was still a long way from learning any of those lessons, however. Instead, I just struggled along, trying to keep afloat.

In the midst of all the family and school drama that made up my junior high years, something surprising happened. I had a couple of classes with a group of girls who all went to the same church. One Monday I overheard them talking about all the fun they'd had the night before at youth group. I didn't own a Bible, and I'd never thought about studying it, but something inside of me wanted to know more. I don't know if I was just yearning for community and thought that this might be a place where

I could fit in or what the reason might have been, but when I got home, I asked my parents if I could start going. To my relief, they said yes.

The first night of attending the youth group wasn't nearly as awkward as I'd expected. Kids from all over Bakersfield attended. Some went to my school, but a lot of them went to other schools around town. I kept going week after week and started making new friends. My parents noticed, especially after I asked them if we could go to church on Sunday morning. While I enjoyed the youth group on Sunday nights, I wanted more. Since I couldn't drive, I needed my parents to take me. And if they were already at the church, I figured we might as well stay, all of us.

To my surprise, when I asked my dad if we could start going to church as a family, he seemed really happy about it. The next Sunday, he and my mom got all of us kids up and we went. We even stuck with it for a few weeks. But eventually the old habits came back, and going to church fell by the wayside. One day I got up the courage to ask my dad why. He told me, "Kyrah, if you're religious, you're religious. You don't have to go to church to prove it." I thought about his answer for a while, but it didn't seem right to me. I didn't go to church to prove anything to anyone. I went because being surrounded by fellow believers gave me peace and community that I didn't have in any other facet of my life. God through the Holy Spirit kept pulling me in and showing me that I was meant to be there. All of this was still pretty new to me, but I believed what I'd heard so far. When I learned what the gospel was one night at youth group and got the big picture about who Jesus was and what He had done for me on the cross, I didn't just believe it. Deep down, I wanted to live for Him.

My faith was put to the test early on. I kept going to church on Sunday mornings and attending youth group on Sunday nights, and I signed up for a small group on Wednesday nights. The church wasn't far from our home, but it certainly wasn't within walking distance. With my dad out of town for work most Wednesdays, my mom had to drive me. I'm one of four kids, we all still lived at home, and all of us had a lot of stuff going on. Between driving us back and forth to different schools and sports practices and my competitive cheer practices, my mom felt like she spent more time in the car than she did in our house. At one point, my siblings and I were in three different schools, and my mom drove us to all of them rather than have us ride the bus. As a stay-at-home mom, she believed it was her job to do everything for us. She wouldn't have had it any other way. However, all the running around took its toll, especially when I'd ask her to take me to church on Sundays and Wednesdays. My mom has never really been into church. I think she only went with my dad those few weeks because she wanted so badly to save her marriage and realized she couldn't do it on her own. But God is not a genie who exists to grant our wishes on our time. When my parents' marriage didn't magically get better, church quickly became something my mom didn't care for. Some weeks all of the driving and constantly being asked to do things for us was too much for her and she'd lose it out of frustration.

But I kept going to church. I can't tell you why. No one encouraged me to do so. Even the friendships I made at church didn't exactly go the way I had hoped, at least not in those junior high years. Twice a year, our youth group went to a Christian camp up in the Sierra Nevada mountains called Hume Lake. Some years, camp felt like being back in the junior high cafeteria. Girls whispered secrets and left me out. They'd walk in front of me and I'd be left behind. Not everyone was like this, but there were enough of them to make me want to wonder if any of them were my real friends. I now realize that most were in that mean-girl phase a lot of girls go through. We all pretty much grew out of it eventually, but at the time, being snubbed by Christian girls I thought were my friends made sticking with church hard to do.

Why didn't I walk away? Looking back, I understand the only answer is God. He was the one constant in my life, without me even realizing it. I didn't fully grasp it at the time, but He became the one place where I truly belonged. I knew He loved me and accepted me exactly as I was. I'll freely admit I didn't read my Bible as much as I should have to really understand my faith. That came later. But I knew what I believed. I loved Jesus and I wanted to live for Him.

2

Remember Me?

KYRAH:

After our breakup, I didn't hear from Kaelin for nearly three years. Outside of that one day in seventh-grade English, I never had him in any of my classes. When we all moved on from junior high to high school, we ended up at different schools.

To be honest, I didn't think much about Kaelin in those three years. Even after a message popped up in my Twitter notifications during my sophomore year of high school telling me Kaelin Edwards was now following me, I didn't start daydreaming about the love we'd shared back in seventh grade. If I remember correctly, I clicked on his profile to see what he looked like now, thought he was cute, and followed him back. I then went back to doing whatever I was doing. I practically lived on Twitter back in 2013. Twitter then was not what Twitter is today. My friends and I used it as a way to talk to everyone in our circle all at once. Some nights we pulled all-nighters, tweeting back and forth to each other. I knew people outside my group of friends could read what we said to each other, but I didn't worry about it. I was fifteen. I didn't think anyone who didn't know me cared that much about what I had to say. That's why I didn't give it much thought when Kaelin started following me. If a guy I knew back in seventh grade wanted to join in the conversation, great.

One tweet did catch my eye, however. It was not actually by Kaelin, but it was about him. A girl I didn't know had tweeted that Kaelin had broken up with her because she wasn't Christian enough. I wasn't exactly sure what she meant by that, but I remember thinking, *Hmmm, Kaelin has to be pretty serious about Jesus for her to post something like that. That's good to know.*

I guess Kaelin followed me a little more closely than I followed him. He tweeted, "Congratulations," to me one day after he saw a photo of me and my new boyfriend on Twitter. Boyfriend is a little strong of a word to describe my relationship with that guy. My friends kept coming up to me and telling me, "I heard he really likes you. Do you like him too?" The guy and I were really great friends, and I told them I thought he was sweet. He never actually asked me to be his girlfriend, but we would text and see each other between classes. One day he held my hand as he walked me to class. I didn't know it, but one of my friends snapped a picture with her phone and sent it to me. I had the bright idea of making it my header on Twitter. I might as well have taken the photo into my parents' room and just showed my dad. A day or two after I made it my Twitter header, he walked into my room and said, "I need your phone."

"Okay," I said, unsure of what was going on.

"And you're not getting it back," he said.

"Wait! What? Why?" I asked.

"I told you no boyfriends until you turn sixteen. Maybe not having your phone for a year will let you know how serious I am," my dad said.

"How am I supposed to talk to my friends?" I asked.

"Use the home phone," my dad said as he turned and walked out of my room.

Who uses their phones to make calls? I thought. I didn't. Thankfully my mom came to my rescue. Sort of. She didn't get my phone back, but she did let me use her phone behind my dad's back to text my friends and talk to them via Twitter. This wasn't unusual. My dad was typically the strict parent, the structured-household parent, while my mom was more laid-back and focused on being our friend. My dad was the disciplinarian who made lots of rules, while my mom often came up with loopholes. With my dad out of town for days at a time, my siblings and I had plenty of days where we were able to bask in my mom's carefree lifestyle. We went shopping with her and picked up Starbucks and did whatever else we wanted. My mom even let me skip first period when I was too tired to get up, and she often picked me up from school early just so the two of us could hang out. My mom sneaking me her phone so I could socialize with my friends fit right into this pattern. It wasn't the same as having my own, but there wasn't a lot I could do about it. To me, my dad was playing the typical dad role; he thought it was unimaginable that his fifteen-year-old daughter could have a crush on a boy. He was being dramatic over a harmless crush, and his actions showed he didn't trust me at all. It's no wonder I felt much closer to my mom.

KAELIN:

Kyrah and I may have gone our separate ways, but I never forgot about her. We followed each other on Instagram and Twitter. I didn't follow her to try to win her back though. Nah. To me, she'd had her chance. Still, my curiosity led me to occasionally check her pages to see what she was up to.

Toward the end of eighth grade, everyone started talking about what high school they would go to. Our school district drew a line that literally went right down the railroad tracks. Which side of the tracks you lived on determined which high school you went to. I didn't know where Kyrah lived, but one of my friends let me know that she was going to the other high school in town. I have to tell you, when I heard that, my heart sank a bit. Part of me always wondered if we might get back together someday, but now that we were going to different schools, I figured that door had closed for good. That was probably a good thing because I changed a lot through junior high and my freshman year of high school. I wasn't much like the guy who was smitten by the chance to spend the last five minutes of the school day hugging my girlfriend. In my mind, I had grown out of that phase. I wanted more freedom and new experiences. My curiosity led me to question nearly everything my parents had taught me when I was younger, and the biggest questions I had all had to do with God. Kyrah's family may not have talked about God, but in my house, everything we did orbited the church.

I did more than just grow up in church. When your dad is the pastor, church is your life, and a huge part of my life was spent in the pews of Rising Star Baptist Church. Every member of our family had a job there. Of course, as the pastor, my dad was in charge. My mom wore a bunch of hats as First Lady, literally and figuratively. In Black churches, the First Lady keeps everyone happy and everything moving along with a smile on her face and while dressed to the nines. At some point, all of my sisters and brothers either served as ushers or sang in the choir, or did both. My siblings organized events and led Bible studies, and my oldest brother even played the organ during the services. As for me, when I was younger, I was too shy to be an usher and choir has never really been my thing. I ended up spending a lot of time up in the sound room with my then brother-in-law. Most Sundays, I split my time between playing on the floor among all the cords and amps and asking my brother-in-law what all the different pieces of machinery did. He explained things to me, which I thought was pretty cool because I was intrigued by how everything worked.

As time went on, I spent less time playing and more time learning how to run the sound system. I still didn't really have an official job at the church until one Sunday when my brother-in-law had to leave the sound room for a few minutes. While he was gone, one of the mics started squeaking. I popped up and fixed it. After that I started taking more and more interest in the tech side of church until eventually I ran the sound room by myself.

Working sound from such a young age gave me a different perspective on the Black church experience. Rather than being up front with my family, fully immersed in worship, I spent my time in the back, alone. While everyone else got swept up in the music and drumbeats and dancing, I had to pay attention to sound levels and tweak microphones. Eventually the sound room was moved up to the second level of the church sanctuary. That meant I also missed out on interacting with other church members. I never formed the kinds of relationships the rest of my family did.

After I became the official sound tech in my early teens, my dad and I met every week to discuss what he wanted in the services from a production standpoint. After a while, those meetings left me disillusioned. Up front I'd hear my dad or an evangelist who came in for a revival service talk about how the service was going to be led by the Holy Ghost, and we weren't going to stop until God said stop. Up in the sound room, I already had the Holy Ghost's schedule printed out right in front of me. To me, that made church services feel a little manipulative. Maybe they weren't, but my doubts about the sincerity of the services played into the ocean of questions already swirling inside of me.

I had questions about everything, from the historical accuracy of the stories in the Bible to how to reconcile science and the miraculous. I had been taught to think for myself, yet when I started to ask questions, I could tell it was a bit of an issue. I had trouble understanding why. All my life, my parents had stressed how I needed to develop a personal faith, but when I tried now, I felt like I got shot down. And personal for me didn't mesh with what personal meant in my charismatic church experience. I watched people have Holy Ghost experiences that touched their emotions, but I wanted to explore the history and theology behind the stories of the Bible. In high school, I got into speech and debate, which taught me more about how to do deductive reasoning. I was exposed to the pathos, ethos, and logos of Aristotle's modes of persuasion used to sway an audience to believe a particular point of view. I applied that to my dad's church, and I could see every rhetorical appeal being used to provide a great church experience. That explained why I felt church was so manipulative. Whether they knew it or not, the leaders used Aristotle's tactics to persuade during services. I know that sounds horrible, but as they were orators and leaders, I expected nothing less. In fact, every person on Earth engages in these modes daily. What I found repulsive was the emphasis on the pathos, or emotion. I wanted the logos, or logic. I didn't want any sappy emotional messages. I yearned for rich expository sermons. I didn't mind the authority structures or experiences people were having so long as they could be logically explained. But when they couldn't, I passed them off as illegitimate hysteria, as nothing more than emotional experiences with no reasonable explanations. And my debate experience taught me that reasonable arguments were everything. The less of them I saw in my church experience, the more I started to challenge my dad's church's teachings.

I vividly remember asking one of my Bible study teachers one Wednesday about Noah's flood. I asked what seemed to me to be a perfectly logical question. "Did the whole earth flood, or only a portion of it, because if the whole earth was underwater, where did the dove Noah released go? How could it find an olive branch since every olive tree had been underwater for months?"

"God simply made the olive tree come back quickly so that the dove could find the branch," she replied. It sounded to me like a prepackaged answer.

"That doesn't make a lot of sense. Olive trees grow at lower elevations, which means if the whole earth was underwater during the flood and the waters were slowly receding, elevations where olives grow had to still be underwater," I replied.

She let out a frustrated sigh, then said, "We will never understand some of the mysteries of the Bible this side of heaven."

When I questioned that statement, she added, "Some things we just have to accept by faith," then said, "Okay, let's move on…"

I looked around the room and was like, *What? Is anyone else hearing this? I thought this was a Bible study. Are you telling me that instead of diving deep into the hard parts of the Bible, I need to stop thinking and fall in line with everyone else? Am I seriously supposed to go along and blindly accept everything you tell me?* I thought this, but I kept my mouth shut. This really wasn't a question for this unsuspecting Wednesday night youth Bible study leader, but a question for my dad. Sometimes I'd ask him serious questions about apparent contradictions in the Bible, but he'd rarely give answers I thought were acceptable.

Eventually I grew tired of the overly simplistic *don't question, just believe* approach to God. How intellectually honest would I be if I questioned every other authority and held their answers up to scrutiny, but then left all discernment at the door the moment I stepped into church? To me, it sounded like someone was hiding something from me, like those on the inside knew this was all a lie but they couldn't let anyone else in on their secret. I felt like I had to be the only one asking these kinds of questions. If no one else was asking, perhaps it was because everyone else who thought for themselves had already discovered that there was nothing to all this God stuff, that it was all a lie. And if it was a lie, I was ready to walk away.

I didn't give up that easily, though. I read and did research and tried to reconcile the faith I heard about in my dad's church with the questions in my own mind. I dove into books and articles from atheists and scientists. I found answers, but those answers pulled me further and further away from the idea of God. All the while, I kept doing sound at my dad's church because, after all, church was the family business. Everyone had to do their part.

In the middle of my journey, my high school Spanish teacher handed me a copy of Lee Strobel's *The Case for Christ*. "You ask a lot of questions about God," she said. "So did the guy who wrote this. I challenge you to read it and honestly consider what he has to say." Challenge accepted. I read it that night and handed it back to her the following day. "That's nothing but a softball book," I told her. "Most of Strobel's arguments have easy explanations that do not require any kind of belief in God. This is a good faith builder for beginners in apologetics, but he doesn't address the latest arguments from academia." Part of my response to the book came from my own arrogance. I felt like I was smarter than the average Joe, especially the average Christian Joe. *The Case for Christ* might answer all their questions, but it didn't answer mine. Not even close.

By this point, I barely considered myself a Christian. My dad and I had some understandable tension in those days. Our conflicting beliefs led us to keep butting heads. I may have stopped asking him questions, but I still had enough intellectual curiosity to keep looking for answers to life's big questions. I wondered why I existed and what the point of life was. Those questions led me to read old philosophers like Friedrich Nietzsche and naturalists like Charles Darwin. I also listened to debates between Christian apologists and atheists on YouTube. "Don't turn into one of those people who are always learning and never able to arrive at a knowledge of the truth," my dad warned. That only made me want to watch that much more. I didn't want to hide from the truth.

A funny thing happened on my way toward totally discrediting Christianity in my mind. Through the books and debates, I discovered that Christian thinkers had been wrestling with these same questions since the beginning of the church. I also observed that the Christian arguments in debates were much more consistent and convincing than their opponents'. In every debate, the deductive reasoning used inevitably led to the cross of Christ. And my pride proved to be no match for God's relentless love and pursuit of me. I still had questions that needed answers, but I could not get away from the love of God expressed in Jesus's dying for me. In the end, that love was irresistible. After years of doubting God and fighting against being told what I was supposed to believe, Jesus became real to me. I chose to follow Him, not because my pastor dad told me I should but because I knew, in the words of John 6:68, I had nowhere else to turn to find real truth. What else could I devote my life to that was going to matter?

I didn't get to that place overnight. However, when I finally came to that place where I had to say that Jesus is real and I want to live for him, I had to take a hard look at a lot of the stuff I was doing. I was very ashamed of a lot of what I saw. I had a girlfriend I'd been dating for eight months while I was figuring myself and faith out. When I came to the place of confessing Jesus was real and I wanted to live for him, I knew one of my first steps into this new life had to be breaking up with her. The problems in that relationship had nothing to do with her. I was the one at fault. Some stuff in that relationship had gotten out of hand because my motives for dating her had all been wrong.

When I honestly examined why I was dating her, I then had to take a hard look at all my romantic relationships and how I'd treated girls. That was rough because I had not been a good guy. God convicted my heart and drove me to my knees over what I had done. You see, I had this gift of gab, and I used it to get what I wanted. And that's how I looked at relationships with girls. It was all about me. I liked getting at girls, but after I got what I wanted, I was disengaged. God put His foot down on me in a big way over that. I needed to get it together. I had to put a gap between me and girls for a while before I hurt someone else. Jesus said that if your right eye causes you to stumble, you need to pluck it out because it's better to go through life with one eye than to have your whole body plunged into hell (Matthew 5:29). I don't think Jesus actually meant for us to go around plucking our eyeballs out of their sockets, but He was telling us to remove from our lives whatever drags us down into doing what we shouldn't be doing. So that's why I not only broke up with my girlfriend but also made up my mind that I wasn't going to pursue any girls until I understood how to properly pursue a sister in Christ.

How do I date the Godly way? I asked myself. Playing games with girls' emotions and looking at the whole dating dynamic as a way of getting what I wanted definitely was not what God wanted for anyone. But what did He want? I looked at my parents' relationship. They got married young and not under the best of circumstances, but they made it work. If I stayed on the path I was on, I could see myself having to get married not under the best of circumstances too. Could I actually see myself marrying any of the girls I'd dated in the past? And if I couldn't, what was I even doing dating them? Wasn't that the ultimate point of dating, to find the one with whom you will spend the rest of your life?

The more I thought about these questions, the more a conviction began to grow in my heart. Even though I was only fifteen, my understanding of the Bible made me decide I should only enter into relationships with the opposite sex that could ultimately lead to marriage—that is, I should date with intention. I also became more and more convinced that God's best is for sex to come after marriage, and I wanted God's best. My parents had preached "no sex before marriage" to my siblings and me, with varying degrees of success. I wanted to change that for my life. By God's grace and through no credit of my own, I had not yet experienced sexual intercourse, and I intended to keep it that way. I decided to date with an eye toward marriage, and I'd wait until marriage to have sex. I firmly believed that's what God wanted for His children. I even boiled my new convictions down to a handy little saying: "I date to marry." But first,

I thought it best not to date at all for a while. Like I said, my track record in the way I'd treated girls hadn't exactly been great so far. I needed a sizable gap to basically do a hard reset on myself.

I'd been in my dating gap for a while, with varying degrees of success, when I saw a picture of Kyrah on social media with her braces off. *Gah, just, gah*, I thought. She was beautiful before but now, whew. I had to reach out to her. But I couldn't. After scrolling through her Twitter page, I saw a photo of her holding hands with another guy. She now had a love interest who was not me. *Good for her*, I thought. *I hope she's happy.* I tweeted at them to congratulate their new relationship. I truly meant what I tweeted. I really was happy for her that she had a guy in her life, even if it wasn't me. However, I'd be lying if I told you that I wasn't even happier when I saw they'd broken up a month later. I wondered what went wrong. I put two and two together and figured he had to have messed up. Bad for him, but good for me. After he dropped the ball, I just knew I could treat her better. I'm no rebound, I decided, so I wanted to give her time to get over this guy. *But what if she takes him back?* I thought. I decided I couldn't wait. This was the chance I'd been waiting on.

3

Rekindled Intentionally

KYRAH:

My phone dinged, telling me someone had just favorited one of my tweets. It was actually my mom's phone since my dad still hadn't given mine back. If my mom knew I was still up at 4 a.m. pulling an all-night Twitter-after-dark session with my friends, she might have taken her phone back. On second thought, probably not. My relationship with my mom changed once I got into high school. We became less like mother and daughter and more like best friends. She let me do pretty much whatever I wanted— within reason—including looking the other way when I stayed up all night tweeting back and forth with my friends.

I glanced down to see which one of my friends had just favorited something I'd tweeted, but none of them had. Instead, it was Kaelin. Over the past few weeks, the two of us had started tweeting back and forth to each other occasionally, but not with any kind of consistency and never in the middle of the night. *What is he doing up so late?* I said to myself, smiling.

I immediately replied to him, "Go to sleep," hoping he'd catch on to what I was really saying. I didn't want him literally to go to sleep. I wanted him to start talking to me.

THIS KIND OF LOVE

He replied right away. "If you're actually speaking to me, then I'm already dreaming."

I gasped and immediately put my hand over my mouth, hoping my parents didn't hear me. With butterflies fluttering in my stomach, I typed, "You dream about me talking to you?"

But he did not reply. I guess he really did go to sleep. My Twitter circle wrapped up our tweet storm a short time later and I went to bed myself. However, as I lay there, I couldn't help but ask myself, *What was that all about?* I hadn't seen Kaelin since junior high, and even though we'd tweeted back and forth to each other a few times since we started following each other on Twitter, it had never been like this and I'd never felt like *that*. He was definitely flirting with me, right? *Does that mean he's interested in me?* I wondered. The whole conversation left me a little confused.

KAELIN:

I thought I gave Kyrah the line of the year. "If you're actually speaking to me, then I'm already dreaming." How could she not take that bait? But she didn't. Her response seemed as if she didn't know I was flirting with her. I may have shut it down for that night, but over the next few weeks I continued to drop subtle hints that I was interested in her.

We exchanged these tweets on August 8. School started soon after, and even though I had made up my mind not to date anyone for a while, I couldn't help but notice some cute freshman girls coming into my high school. I had a rule back then: two above and two below. That meant I'd date girls two years older than me and two years younger than me, but nothing beyond that. I was a junior. Even if I didn't plan on asking any of them out, what could it hurt to talk to a couple of these freshmen? I even went to a back-to-school dance, but I told myself before I went that I wasn't going to get out on the dance floor and start doing the usual bumping and grinding that I did when I was the old Kaelin. I was just there to be sociable. However, I got a little too sociable because I found myself out on the dance floor and the old Kaelin came back in all his glory. God convicted my heart so strongly that night. I call that the last night of the old Kaelin. You might be thinking, *What did you do that was so bad? Are you telling me that people shouldn't dance?* No, I'm not saying that at all. But there's a difference between dancing and stirring up a fire inside that's hard to control. I'd fought that fire before. I didn't want to light it up again.

In between the dances and seeing the new girls at school, I kept thinking about Kyrah. I still hadn't seen her since seventh grade, but something about her kept drawing me to her. I didn't have her number, so the only way I could talk to her was *subtly* through Twitter. Unfortunately, she didn't always catch my "subtle tweets," or what we called "subtweets." A subtweet is a tweet sent out publicly addressed to no one but secretly for someone. It's like publicly writing in code hoping the person the message is for picks it up and knows it's for them. When I was in high school, that was our fun way of *secretly* admiring someone *publicly* and also finding out if they admired you back. That's some vital information because I needed to know she was interested before I made the first direct move.

Kyrah was a cheerleader at her school, and the first game of the season was coming up that Friday night. I wanted to see Kyrah, but I couldn't just go to her house. And not going to the same school made it even more challenging. I was beginning to see that the football game was going to be my best bet. But I didn't want to show up without her looking forward to *possibly* seeing me. That's why I went fishing first. I tweeted out, "Oomf [one of my followers] has me deeply confused."

A few minutes later, I received the reply I was looking for. Kyrah subtweeted, "Me?"

I didn't reply. I didn't need to. I saw what I needed to see.

The next day I tweeted, "If things worked the way I wanted them to, I would not be single and oomf would be taken." I also favorited one of her tweets about the upcoming football game. And then I sat back and waited to see what she might say.

It took a day, but then she subtweeted, "Do you like me or not? I don't understand." I did not immediately reply. Instead, I waited. The next day she removed all doubt and tweeted, "**Kaelin Edwards** better be coming to the game tomorrow." I favorited that tweet, which made her say, "Does this mean you're going orrrr?" Again, I didn't reply. She'd get her answer the next day.

KYRAH:

I had butterflies fluttering in my stomach while cheering at the first football game of the year. I didn't wear my glasses while cheering out of fear they'd fly off during a tumbling pass, and I didn't own contacts, so I couldn't see if Kaelin was in the crowd or not. He had been so secretive in his tweets that even though I was pretty sure he was there, there was no way I could know for sure.

At least not while the game was going on.

After the game ended, I was walking with my friends toward the one gate everyone has to go through to leave the football field and head toward the parking lot. It passes right by the concession stand. And that's when I saw Kaelin walking toward me. My first reaction was to turn the other way. I mean, I wanted to see him, but I did not want to see him. My friend closest to me looked ahead and saw Kaelin. "Is that the guy you've been talking to on Twitter?"

"Yeah," I said. "I can't believe he came."

"Aren't you glad he did?" she asked.

"I don't know yet."

The closer we got, the more nervous I became. If you watch our story-time video where we go into even more detail, you know he was just as nervous as I was. I asked my friend, "Can I borrow your phone?"

"Why?"

"I need to text my mom and make sure she's the one who picks me up. If my dad sees me talking to a guy…"

"Sure," my friend said.

After I texted my mom, I handed the phone back to my friend and said, "Do not leave my side."

She agreed, but as soon as we got up to Kaelin, she left me. Kaelin's friend disappeared as well, leaving Kaelin and me alone to have a very awkward conversation. I say awkward because not only had we not seen each other since seventh grade, but we also hadn't talked since I'd broken up with him. We were twelve or thirteen back then. I had just turned sixteen. A lot happens between your thirteenth and sixteenth birthdays. I had changed a lot, and I was sure he had too. What were we supposed to talk about now?

"I told you I was going to be here," Kaelin said with a smile when I first walked up to him.

"Hmmm, I don't remember you saying that," I said with a little laugh.

He laughed. "Well, basically," he said. Or something like that. To be honest, I was so nervous that it is hard to remember. It wasn't just seeing him for the first time in forever that made me so nervous. My parents were going to pick me up after the game. If my dad pulled up and saw me talking to a boy, I had no idea what he might do. "Can I walk you to your car?" he asked.

"Okay," I said, "but I didn't drive. My parents are going to pick me up." As I said this, I prayed my mom saw my text.

KAELIN:

When I saw Kyrah walking toward me, my heart leaped. *This could be my future wife*, I imagined. While walking Kyrah to the parking lot, I tried to play it cool. She told me her mom was going to pick her up, which made me even more focused because nothing moves things forward in a relationship quite like a good impression on parents. Kyrah and I stood talking in the parking lot for what seemed like less than a minute when a big Tahoe pulled up. The driver's side window slowly went down. I saw a woman wearing dark glasses behind the wheel. "Kaelin, this is my mom," Kyrah said.

I smiled. "Nice to meet you, Mrs. Stewart."

Kyrah's mom laughed. "You can call me Karen. Nice to meet you, Kaelin. Do you need a ride?" she asked.

"No, thank you," I said respectfully. "I drove. I parked right over there."

"So you drive already?" she asked.

"Oh yeah," I said. "Have to get to work somehow," I added, motioning over toward my black Expedition. I hoped to gain extra points by getting a chance to mention I worked two jobs, one as a teller at a credit union and one at a local fast-casual Mexican restaurant. I'd rather talk about my two jobs than explain how I was driving with my permit and my parents' blessing, not a license. But Kyrah's mom didn't take the bait, so I didn't get the points and she didn't get the explanation.

After turning down a ride, I walked Kyrah over to the passenger side of the car and opened the door for her. I wanted to hug her, but I didn't dare do it in front of her mom. "It was good seeing you again, Kyrah," I said.

"You too," Kyrah said.

KYRAH:

Kaelin showed up for the rest of my home football games that fall. We started talking more, but because I still didn't have a phone, we had to do most of it through Twitter. Even with that, I had to be very careful because my dad kept such a close eye on my social media life. I may have been sixteen, and that was the age at which he'd said I'd be allowed to date, but there was more to his rules than a number. Any boy who wanted to date me had to meet him first. I wasn't ready for Kaelin to meet my dad. More importantly, I didn't think my dad was ready to meet Kaelin or any other guy. Eventually he'd have to, but I wanted to give this relationship a little more time before I put Kaelin through that.

One day Kaelin sent me a DM. "I'd like to get together sometime so that we can talk," he said.

"Okay," I said, but I didn't know how that might work. "But you know my parents are really strict about that."

"Not a date," Kaelin replied. "I just want to talk where we'd have more time and more privacy than the ten minutes after a football game."

"I'll let you know," I said.

A couple of weeks later, he called me on our home phone. "Would now work? Maybe we could go for a walk or sit outside, just to talk."

My mom was gone and my dad was about to leave for work, so I told Kaelin, "Sure, I can make it work." My dad overheard the call and asked what was going on. I lied and said, "Oh that was my friend; she's going to come over for a little bit." My dad said okay, but he must have seen through my lie because he took *forever* to actually leave the house. He kept finding one excuse after another to keep from walking out the door. My heart started racing. If Kaelin came up to the house and my dad saw him...I didn't want to think about what might happen.

But my dad kept hanging around and hanging around. I had to do something to make sure Kaelin didn't walk up to my door. That's when I came up with a great plan. I crawled out my window and snuck out to the front of the house. Sure enough, I saw Kaelin parked at the end of the street. He started to get out of his car, but I motioned for him to stay where he was.

A moment later, my dad walked outside to get in his truck. He saw me standing around in front of the house and gave me a very suspicious look. "What are you doing out here?" he asked.

"Just waiting for my friend," I said, trying to sound as casual as possible.

My dad still seemed suspicious, but he said okay, and then got in his truck and left.

I waited until I was sure he wasn't going to circle back around the block, then motioned for Kaelin to come on over. "Is everything okay?" I asked.

"Can we go on a walk and talk?" Kaelin asked with almost a solemn tone. I'd never seen him quite like this.

"Sure. What do you want to talk about?" I asked.

"I really like you, but I don't want to waste your time or my time," Kaelin said.

"Okay," I said, uncertain where this conversation was about to go.

"I want to pursue a relationship with you and see where this goes, but before we do, I need to make something clear," Kaelin said.

Now I was really confused. Was he about to tell me something about his last girlfriend? Or maybe something was wrong with him? I had no idea. No boy had ever talked with me like this.

"I date to marry, and I plan to marry someone who shares my faith and values," Kaelin said.

"Okay," I said, not really sure what he meant by that.

"That means I don't want to date anyone I can't see myself marrying, but also, when I date, I want to take this seriously and not play games. I've already seen how games don't work," he said.

"With your ex?" I asked. He nodded. "So, what exactly happened with her?" I asked.

"I'm not ready to go into detail about that right now. It's nothing against her. Let's just say I made some mistakes," he said. "And I've changed a lot since then. I'm not the same guy I was when I dated her."

"Okay," I said.

"Kyrah, if I pursue you, I don't see this potentially as just a 'high school' relationship. I want to get to know you and who you are and what matters most to you and what you want to do with your life. If what you want to do with your life is completely different from where I see my life going, then there's no sense in us dating. That doesn't mean I wouldn't still like you a lot, but I'd rather us figure these things out now, at the start, than later on. Does that make sense?"

"I agree," I said, and I meant it. I'd never thought about a dating relationship like this before, but it made perfect sense to me. I remember one of my small group leaders at church talking about how we didn't need to be dating and getting into serious relationships while we were so young. She had encouraged us to date for short periods of time instead. I don't remember her exact reasons for this, as I wasn't even allowed to date at the time. I've always been extremely shy and slow to open up. I needed someone who would be sensitive and okay with taking things slow because they were in it for the long run. The way Kaelin spoke to me that night with forthrightness showed that he was already looking out for his and my best interests. He wanted to know me and build a foundation for a possible marriage. At the time, I wasn't able to fully put it all into words, but his honesty and directness were comforting.

"I'm not in a hurry when it comes to relationships. I'm not interested in 'using' you. I like you a lot and I respect you, and I want to get to know you more. I just don't want to lead you on if we're not on the same page. To be clear, as a Christian, I'm saving myself physically for my future wife. I respect myself and I don't want to put myself in a place where I might do something I'll regret. Like I said, I'd like to pursue a relationship with you, but only if that's something you're interested in. If not, then that's fine. I'd rather us end this before we get started so that neither of us ends up breaking the other's heart," Kaelin said.

"I like you too," I said with a smile. "I'm a Christian and I agree with you about waiting until marriage. So I guess let's see where this goes," I said, which made Kaelin smile. "But…you know you have to meet my dad before this can go anywhere."

"I'm not worried about meeting your dad," he said.

You should be, I thought. *You really should be.*

4

Detoured

KAELIN:

My intentions talk with Kyrah went great. Before our talk, I had kept myself pretty guarded. While I couldn't wait to get to know her more, I also did not want to start falling hard for her without the possibility of a future together. I'm not saying I already knew she was the ONE, but I believed she *could* be. Only time would tell.

Unfortunately, even after our talk, we didn't get to start dating or even talking on a regular basis. She didn't have a phone, not since her dad had taken it away more than a year before. That meant we couldn't text or call each other. Even though she was sixteen now, and by her dad's rules technically allowed to date, we still didn't know the process of actually gaining his approval. In the meantime, while we figured out how to properly introduce me to her dad, Kyrah didn't want me to call their home phone because he might answer, and that would make a horrible first impression. My parents figured out about one of my sister's boyfriends through a late-night call. Seeing how they reacted made me never want to be anyone's secret. Kyrah's mom agreed to let me come over to their house for short, clandestine visits behind her dad's back, but I could not go inside their house and I couldn't stay long. I felt uneasy about the sneaking around, but every time I asked about meeting her dad, Kyrah always told me, "I don't think he's ready."

"Why not?" I asked. I was eager to meet him. My high school class voted me "best to take home to meet your parents," and for good reason. I knew I could make a great impression on him. I had a way with parents.

"You don't understand about my dad," she replied. "He's really strict with me. He has fake social media accounts that he uses to read everything I put online without me knowing it. That's how I lost my phone. He saw the picture of me holding hands with a guy last year, and I haven't had a phone since."

"I don't want to disrespect him trying to go behind his back, but I really would like to meet him."

"You can't just come over and meet him. The timing has to be right to catch him in the right mood."

"When will that be?" I asked.

"I don't know. Soon," Kyrah said.

"How soon?" I asked.

"I don't know," Kyrah said.

With meeting her dad on indefinite hold, I had to settle for only seeing her at football games and when I just *happened* to be in the neighborhood. I went to every one of her home football games and every away game that was in town. It wasn't my school, but I may as well have had season tickets. I sat through the entire game just to grab five or ten minutes with her after it was over. It wasn't much, but at least it was something, until even that came to a crashing end. Literally.

I had turned sixteen at the beginning of the summer that Kyrah and I started talking again. My parents had given me a car for my birthday, a black 1998 Eddie Bauer edition Ford Expedition. My new car was actually my mom's old car, one she got right after I was born, but I didn't care. I loved everything about my car, except the license plate. My mom had her own personalized tag, which was now my personalized tag. It fit her. It didn't fit me. My friends all made fun of me when they saw me rolling up with my "SISTER E" plates. I may have had embarrassing license plates, but I also had something hardly anyone else had, and that was my own car. I just smiled as I cruised by them walking home in the hot Bakersfield sun.

Even though I had my own car, there was still that one important thing I did not yet have: a driver's license. I had my permit, but you needed to have it for six months before you could take the behind-the-wheel driver's test for your license. I was only four months in. Even though I didn't have my license, my parents let me go ahead and start driving. My dad put it like this: "I'd rather you drive yourself without a license than ride in a car with your friends." It wasn't that he didn't trust their driving. He didn't trust them. My dad was all too familiar with stories of guys whose lives basically ended because they were with a friend who did something stupid and ended up in trouble with the law. Besides, when you're Black, it seems it's guilt by association. It feels like the police don't care who did what, and if they pull over a car full of Black dudes, they seem to make assumptions that sometimes don't end well for those in the car. I've seen it happen before, and I was not interested in becoming another statistic. And my friends could not ride with me. No exceptions. Again, guilt by association applies whether you are the driver or a passenger.

My dad also taught me what to do when I was pulled over by the police. He said *when*, not *if*. My dad is a pastor and well respected in the community, but even he doesn't get a pass. "Take out yo' license and registration and lay 'em on the dash so the cops can see," he told me. "Then roll every window down and put both of yo' hands on the steering wheel where they can see 'em. Ask permission and announce before you remove yo' hands from the steering wheel to do anything." Even before I started driving, one of my sisters clued me in on how I had to be careful about how I carried myself. "You ain't a cute little boy no more," my sister told me when I hit a growth spurt around the age of thirteen. "You look just like any other Black dude out here. You gotta work to make yo'self look less intimidating. You don't even gotta be doing anything to be looked at suspiciously."

I took my sister's advice to heart without waiting to find out if her warnings were based on fact or not. Everything I ever did, said, or wore was done in a way to appear more disarming. Again, I didn't wait to see if my fears were unfounded. I didn't want to become the example that tested the system. To be honest, the warnings didn't make me angry or sad. This was just the understood reality for those who looked like me.

This reality was tested one Tuesday morning while I was driving down Buena Vista Road on my way to school. I was caught up in a long line of traffic at a red light right next to a Taco Bell. The light finally turned green, and I had just moved my foot from the brake to the gas when I heard a loud smack, which was followed by a second SMACK! My neck snapped forward and my head hit the steering wheel and my heart dropped because I was driving without a license. Out of the corner of my eye, I saw red and blue lights flash, and then I heard the sirens. I prayed it wasn't who I thought it was, but it was just my luck that a police car was parked in the Taco Bell parking lot and was immediately on the scene.

I put my Expedition into park and got out to survey the damage. My car didn't look that bad, and I considered just driving away but thought better of it. The car behind me was a mess. Both the front and rear ends were smashed in. Apparently, that car got rear-ended by a car going around forty, which then pushed it into my car with enough force to mess my car up as well.

The police car from the Taco Bell pulled up next to us.

I called my dad. He didn't answer.

A policeman got out of his car. He looked the scene over and walked straight to me. "Are you okay?"

"Yes. I think so."

"If your car can move, I need you to pull it into the parking lot over there while we sort this all out," he said.

"Yes, sir," I said. I got back into my car and immediately tried calling my dad again. I hid my phone because talking on a cell phone while driving is illegal in California, but then again, so is driving without a license. My dad didn't answer. I parked my car and sat there for a moment trying to get my story together. My dad finally called me back. I broke the news to him quickly: "I just got into an accident on Buena Vista Road by the Taco Bell."

"Imma be right there," my dad said. We lived literally two minutes away, so I knew my dad would be there soon.

I hung up and climbed out of the car as the officer walked back over to me. "I need to see your license."

"Oh, I wasn't driving," I lied, frozen and suddenly out of breath. Every nightmare story I'd heard or watched on the news about a Black man interacting with the police flashed through my mind. That didn't stop me from lying.

"You weren't?" the officer said, eyeing me suspiciously.

"No. I don't have my license yet. I have my permit. But my dad was driving, not me."

"Where is your dad?" I could tell by the look on his face that he didn't believe me.

"At the Taco Bell. He'll be back in a minute."

"Okay," the officer said.

Then my dad pulled up in his car, jumped out, and asked, "What happened?"

The policeman answered the question. "Your son was in an accident." Then he looked at me. "Why did you lie?" he asked.

Another police officer pulled up. I started to panic. My dad stepped in and said something about how I only have a permit but that I would take my driver's test in a month and that we only lived two miles away and I was on my way to school, and then he tried to convince the police officers that the law allowed me to drive under these circumstances.

The police didn't buy it for a second. More officers arrived. I felt like we were surrounded. I braced myself for the worst. But the worst of the worst did not happen. The first officer gave both my father and me a citation, me for driving without a license and my father for allowing it. The officer let us know we'd have a court date, then sent us on our way. My dad arranged for my car to be taken to our house, and he drove me to school. We talked a little in the car, but both of us were too much in shock over what might have happened to say much. I went to school but only made it through one class before all my anxiety hit a level that meant I could not concentrate. I had to go home.

When I finally got home, all I could think about was how all the freedom I enjoyed with my car was now over. I thought I'd have to wait another two years before I could take my driver's test. How could I have any kind of life without a license? How would I get to work? How would I pursue anything with Kyrah without one? We barely got to see each other as it was. No car meant no driving to her house and no dating her once her dad gave us the green light—if he'd ever give us the green light. I didn't know what to do next.

When my dad came home that day, we came up with a way to maybe get me out of this mess. I'd go ahead and take my driver's test as scheduled since I already had the appointment before the accident. Then we'd show the judge I now had my license when we got to court in the hope of the judge letting me keep it. What seemed like a great plan never even materialized because I failed my behind-the-wheel driving test with fly-ing colors. I screwed up a turn that involved a bike lane, which made me take a different route back to the DMV. When we finally arrived back, the instructor in my car notified me that my reroute meant an automatic disqualification.

Thankfully, all of the schemes to try to find a way to wiggle out of this didn't matter in the end. I appeared before the judge and pleaded guilty. My sentence: a $25 fine. I took my driver's test a second time a couple of weeks later and passed. The insurance company totaled my Expedition, even though it was still drivable. We got it fixed and gave it to my sister and still had enough left over to buy me a Ford Contour from a family friend. I named my car Grace. Every day I climbed in it, I thought about the grace the judge showed me and the grace of God to provide favor in a situation where we deserved to suffer the consequences. The way everything turned out reminded me that I needed to tell the truth, lean on God, and leave the results up to Him, rather than lie to try to save my skin. I learned God's grace is enough, but I also learned that I have to conduct myself wisely around people. Some people may still make assumptions about me because of the color of my skin, but I choose to control what I can control. Of course, some days that reality makes me upset, and now that I'm a father of boys myself, I think about how I'll have to prepare them for these kinds of moments. Maybe, by God's grace, when they grow into young men, I won't need to anymore.

5

Meet the Parents

KYRAH:

I was so nervous to tell my dad about Kaelin. He had always said, "No boys…no boys…no boys!" Then I turned sixteen and that should have opened the door for me to have a boyfriend, but I knew he wasn't ready. I wasn't sure if he wanted me to wait to have a boyfriend until I was mature enough to handle it or if he just didn't like the idea of me dating, period. I was worried he would think I only wanted to bring Kaelin around because I was eager to start dating literally anyone now that I was sixteen. That wasn't the case—it just worked out that I reconnected with Kaelin just as I was old enough. Kaelin kept asking me when he could meet my dad because we wanted our relationship to move forward. I continually put him off. "I don't think this is the right time," I said.

"When will it be?" Kaelin asked. We had the same conversation nearly every time we talked, which wasn't that often since I still didn't have a phone. Kaelin wanted to be able to pick me up and take me on dates, and I wanted him to be able to come to my house to hang out. But that couldn't happen until Kaelin met my dad. It was important to both of us that Kaelin make a good first impression because I planned on bringing him around often. The last thing we wanted was for my dad to come home unexpectedly and Kaelin to be there all cozy on the couch. We wanted to be respectful of my dad's wishes, but it was hard because we were so ready to actually be in a relationship. We'd sometimes go more than a week without seeing or speaking to each other. When we finally did, Kaelin always asked again, "Do you know when your dad will be comfortable meeting me? Does he know about me yet? As long as I'm a secret, we can't really progress past this friendship."

"I don't know," I said. "Soon, I hope."

"How soon?" Kaelin pressed.

"I don't know," I said. Then I asked, "Aren't you even a little bit nervous about meeting my dad?"

Kaelin smiled. "Not at all," he said.

"Why not?" I asked.

"I'm pretty good with parents," Kaelin said.

"Well I'm nervous," I said. I knew I needed to talk to my dad about Kaelin, but I didn't know how he'd react, since every time I had ever brought up boys, my dad had shot me down. "It's my job to protect you," my dad had explained when I was younger. "I know what guys are like and what they are after and that's not going to happen to my baby girl," he had told me. I didn't know if my now being sixteen changed anything in his mind, so I put off talking to him about Kaelin. But the longer I put it off, the more I was afraid Kaelin would get tired of waiting and move on.

Football season ended. Fall turned into winter. The fall quarter ended, and we were both on Christmas break. "I think it's time you tell your dad about me," Kaelin told me. "Your mom likes me and is okay with us talking. How much could they differ?"

"That's because my mom isn't as strict as my dad. Maybe you can come over on Christmas. He'll be in a great mood then," I replied.

"Perfect," Kaelin said. "I'm ready."

Christmas Day came. My brother and sisters and my parents were all together and happy. After we opened our presents, my little sisters spent the rest of the day playing with their new toys. But I couldn't relax. I needed to tell my dad that a boy wanted to come over and meet him. *He's not my boyfriend*, I planned to say. *But he'd like to take me out on a date, with your permission.* I kept rehearsing the lines over and over in my head. Even though it was December 25 and cold, I was sweating and so nervous. Every worst-case scenario ran through my head. I imagined my dad getting mad at me for not saying anything about Kaelin earlier and then telling me I could never speak to Kaelin again. I had good reason to think that because every time I had talked to my dad about another guy before I turned sixteen, he had shot me down. Every. Single. Time.

Finally, I worked up the nerve to approach my dad. "Hey, Dad," I said, "there's something I want to talk to you about."

"What's up?" he replied.

"There's this boy who is my friend. I've known him since seventh grade, and I want you to meet him," I said.

"Is it Kaelin?" my dad asked.

My heart stopped. "You know about Kaelin?" I said.

"Your mom told me about him when she met him after one of your football games. She seems to think he's a nice kid. Sure. Invite him over. I'd love to meet him."

"How about today?" I asked.

"Um, I don't think that will work. This is a family day and it's already late. But I'm off tomorrow. He can come over then."

I let out a long sigh when I walked out of the room. I couldn't believe I'd been so afraid to tell my father something *he already knew!*

44

KAELIN:

I wasn't really nervous the day I drove over to Kyrah's house to meet her father for the first time. If anything, I took winning his approval as a challenge I was ready to conquer. I had an advantage in that Kyrah was not introducing me as her boyfriend. Even though I liked her a lot, the two of us were still at the rekindling-our-friendship stage, not the boyfriend/girlfriend stage. Not being introduced as her boyfriend took the pressure off me. If her dad did not think I was the right guy to date his daughter, I'd respect his opinion, and Kaelin and Kyrah as a couple would end before we could even get started. He knew Kyrah much better than I did, and I trusted his discretion. If he told me to get lost, maybe that meant he saw something in me that made me a bad match for his daughter. That didn't mean I'd like his decision, but if he was going to put a stop to us, I'd rather him do it now before Kyrah and I both had fully fallen for each other. I'd rather get hurt a little now than end up totally devastated later on.

I parked on the street and walked up to Kyrah's house. *This could be the beginning of our story*, I thought as I stepped onto their porch. My parents have a great story of how they got together. (Spoiler alert: My mom didn't like my dad at first. She only went out with him the first time as a joke but ended up falling in love with him.) *This could be a story we tell our kids someday*, I thought before I knocked on her door.

Then the door opened veeeerrrrry slowly. I was shocked as this huge shadow emerged in the doorway. As the door opened fully, the light cast a silhouette on a bear of a man. The two of us were close to the same height, but he was literally twice my size.

I took a deep breath and stood up straight. "Hi, I'm Kaelin, Kyrah's friend," I said.

"Kaelin, nice to meet you. Come on in," the bear said as he opened the door and stuck out his hand.

"It's nice to meet you, Mr. Stewart." I shook his hand, which had to be twice the size of mine. *He could crush me*, I thought. "I appreciate you letting me come over today," I said. I stepped inside and looked around for a moment. Kyrah's little sisters were peeking in from the hall. The moment they noticed me looking at them, they took off squealing and giggling.

"Have a seat," Kyrah's dad said, motioning toward the sofa. He then sat down directly across from me. Kyrah sat down next to me. I hadn't noticed her in the room until then because I was so focused on her father. *Tonight is about winning over Papa Bear*, I thought to myself. Her mom sat down by her dad.

"So, Kaelin, tell me about yourself," Kyrah's dad said. *Gladly*, I thought. I'd had this speech ready for months. I told them that I was the youngest of six kids and that my dad was a pastor. Because I knew Kyrah's family didn't really go to church, I watched for a reaction to that last one. They didn't seem to mind, which was a good sign.

KYRAH:

Kaelin is a pastor's kid, so I knew my parents would see his family as extremely religious. My family was basically the opposite. I didn't know how my mom and dad would react to this super Christian boy I'd brought home to meet them. I doubted my mom or dad would say anything to Kaelin's face. If they objected to him being so religious, I'd hear about it later.

My dad then asked Kaelin questions like where he was working and what kind of plans he had for college and what career path he wanted to take after that. You know, the serious dad questions. Kaelin talked about how he hoped to go to Pepperdine and go on to law school or pursue an MBA after that. Some of this was news to me. I'm glad my parents didn't turn to me and ask what I planned to do after high school. *College?* would have been my answer. Beyond that, I had no idea.

I don't remember who brought up the next subject, whether it was

Kaelin or my dad, but I froze when Kaelin said, "I would like to ask your daughter out on a date." I looked over at my mom and dad. While they didn't smile when he said this, they didn't look angry or upset. *Maybe this is going to work out all right*, I thought.

"You want to ask her out?" my dad asked. "I thought Kyrah said you were just friends."

"That's right, sir. We're just friends, but with your permission, I would like for the two of us to see more of each other so that we can figure out if there might be something more between us."

My dad sat back and looked over at Kaelin for a moment. Then he said, "We'll see." My heart sank, but at the same time I was hopeful. At least my dad hadn't said no.

Then Kaelin told my parents what he had told me a couple of months earlier when we had gone on our walk in the park. "Great…but to assure you, just so you know my intentions…," Kaelin continued, "I'm not looking to take advantage of Kyrah or play games with her emotions. I take dating very seriously." He paused for a moment, then added, "I date to marry. I am not saying that Kyrah and I are going to get married someday or anything like that. But what I am saying is that I want the two of us to really get to know each other in a relationship that could potentially last through high school and college and ultimately could result in marriage. Who knows if that will happen, but I think we should approach dating with an openness to that possibility."

To my great relief, neither my mom nor my dad seemed fazed by what Kaelin had said. My dad simply asked, "Why Kyrah?"

KAELIN:

Why Kyrah? I could give him a million answers. "She's beautiful both inside and out," I said. "I admire her sense of self-worth and the convictions that she holds. That's what intrigues me the most about her—her character. We've been friends again for a few months, but it's clear that our values align and that we share the same goal: to date with the intention of marriage and to save ourselves for that day." I paused for a moment after saying this. Looking back, I don't know if Kyrah's parents were relieved or if they thought I was really naive. At the time, I thought they had to admire us for making such a bold decision that went against the tide. I did not know that Kyrah's mom and dad didn't get married until their third child was on the way.

I talked for a while longer about how Kyrah also had an innocence about her and a softness. I remembered the first time I heard her talk. That voice melted me. "That's why I am interested in going on this journey with her," I said with all the seriousness a sixteen-year-old kid can muster.

Her dad nodded and listened. We kept talking for a while longer. He asked more questions, and I answered every one. I kept waiting to hear the words, "Okay, you can ask her out," but they never came. He did, however, seem to approve of me. I was thrilled with that. I knew I'd make a good impression.

The "can I date your daughter?" conversation ended, and Kyrah's sisters drifted back into the room. Now this had become a social visit. Maybe I should have left right then, but I didn't. Her dad and I talked about sports for a while. I told him that I'd played football in junior high and my freshman year of high school but that the 6 a.m. workouts, along with three hours of practice after school every day, had made it hard to play ball and focus on my grades. "I plan on going to college," I shared, "and I'd like to get an academic scholarship. Dedicating that much time to football isn't going to make that happen. Besides, we literally lost every game my last year, so dropping it was an easy choice to make," I said.

"Do you play any sports now?" Kyrah's dad asked.

"Track. Practices are a lot shorter and I like it being an individual sport. That way, win or lose, I know it's on me," I said.

Kyrah's dad nodded, taking it all in. Before he could ask another question, Kyrah's sister Kimora interrupted us and asked me to play dolls with her. What could I say but yes?

I sort of lost track of time until my mom texted me telling me to get home. "You've been there long enough. Don't wait to be asked to leave," she said. Before I left my house, my mom had given some advice about how to conduct myself at the Stewarts' house. My mom and dad had been on the other end of the conversation enough times to know what makes a good impression on parents and what doesn't.

Even after my mom's text, I couldn't just leave. No, I had to wrap this up and leave a great impression without messing up everything I'd spent the last few hours building. Out of respect, I thanked her parents for having me over, hugged her mom, and shook her dad's hand. I said goodbye to Kyrah and her siblings, then headed for the door as her dad escorted me out. No hugs, kisses, or handshakes between Kyrah and me. After all, we were nothing more than "friends."

I drove home thinking I'd nailed this. I expected Kyrah to contact me that night to tell me that her dad loved me and had said that of course I could date his daughter. But she didn't. A few days passed. Kyrah finally gave me the verdict. He hadn't said yes, but he also hadn't said no. "Basically, my dad said you can come over and see me as long as he is at home," she said. "And," she added very excitedly, "I got a new phone!" While this wasn't exactly the news I'd hoped for, I was still very happy to be further than I had been.

KYRAH:

After Kaelin formally met my parents, he thought it was time for me to meet his. I'd briefly met them when I met Kaelin at his school for a homecoming dance early in the school year. My mom took me, and my dad was fine with me going since I told him I was meeting a friend there. It wasn't a date since Kaelin didn't have his car and couldn't have picked me up even if he'd wanted to. His mom and dad dropped him off at the school. I was there when he got out, so I met his parents in the same way Kaelin met my mom in the parking lot after a football game. But that wasn't an official "meeting," and I did not have an actual conversation with them. Kaelin believed it was time that happened. "Hey, if I had to go through all of that and meet your parents, you have to meet mine," he told me over and over.

However, meeting Kaelin's parents was very different for me than meeting mine had been for him. I didn't just have to meet the parents. I had to meet his older sisters too. Kaelin is the youngest of six. His oldest sister is closer to my mom's age than to mine, and that was only one of his older sisters, something Kaelin constantly reminded me about in the days before I was supposed to meet his family. "You know I have sisters…," he said in a way that made it sound like they were going to come after me with a ton of questions. I did not look forward to being interrogated. I hate being around strangers, and I hate talking about myself. Talking to strangers about myself—that was the last thing I wanted to do. But I didn't have a choice.

The big day came on a Saturday. His family was having a big birthday celebration or something like that. Some of the details are fuzzy because I was so nervous. Kaelin drove to my house to pick me up, then took me to his parents' house. We went into the house through the kitchen, where his mom was working on a meal. "Hey, Mom, you remember my friend Kyrah," he said.

His mom said something like, "Oh hey, Kyrah. I'm so glad you could come over today."

I don't remember her exact words, but I will never forget that before she was finished talking, Kaelin had disappeared. I went to sit down on the couch and when I looked up, he was gone! Then his oldest sister walked in. My heart jumped. The cross-examination was about to begin. *Who are you? Why do you want to date my little brother?* All sorts of questions jumped into my head. I kept waiting for Kaelin to walk back in at any moment and rescue me, but he never did.

"Hey, Kyrah. So nice to finally meet you," Kenisha said before sitting down next to me. She was kind and talked to me like I'd known her forever. Instead of interrogating me, his mom and sister made me feel like family.

Finally, Kaelin came back in with a mischievous smile on his face. "How's it going in here?" he asked.

I wanted to go off on Kaelin for leaving me like that. Later, when we talked about it, he jokingly mentioned it was payback for me leaving him in the living room when he met my parents. I told him I hadn't purposely left him to fend for himself and that I was sorry for leaving him. He apologized to me as well.

Now that we'd both met each other's parents, I felt like our relationship could now move out of the glorified friendship category to something more. But what? I wasn't exactly sure, and Kaelin didn't make things much clearer with the stand he took to prove our relationship was completely different from the normal high school romance. Since I had never had a serious boyfriend before, I went along with it. Yet, at the same time, I had to wonder, *Is he even my boyfriend?* The whole thing was way more confusing than it should have been.

6

Where Do We Stand?

KAELIN:

Meeting Kyrah's dad went a lot better than I thought it would. But even after running that gauntlet and winning his approval of sorts, I did not want to ask Kyrah to be my girlfriend. My reasons had nothing to do with her, and I certainly was not afraid of being teased by my friends and my sisters like I had been back in seventh grade. I wanted everyone to know that I was pursuing Kyrah. Why wouldn't I? She was beautiful and smart and just about perfect in every way. I couldn't believe she was even single by the time I'd come back around.

But, no matter how much I liked Kyrah, I did not want to bring the pressure of the labels of boyfriend and girlfriend into our budding relationship, especially since we were still getting to really know each other. I had seen our peers in high school load those labels with entitlement to certain privileges that Kyrah and I believed should be reserved for marriage. People in our schools thought *officially* being boyfriend and girlfriend was a form of real commitment that made it okay for them to act like husband and wife. Put simply, people used those labels as a justification to start having sex. I hated that shallow relationship framework and rejected the expectation that my relationship should fit into it. I wanted a connection built on friendship, not lust; on patience, not an inability to control ourselves. I believed anyone thinking with their mind and not their pants had to see how shallow these relationships built on lust were. The proof lay in how quickly they all ended. The typical relationship in our schools started with titles. I wanted to start with trust.

KYRAH:

My youth group leaders talked a lot about how we should save ourselves for marriage, and I agreed, but my real reason for being so strongly against sex before marriage stemmed from my fear of vulnerability. I remember having a conversation with one of my friends in high school during which I said, "I can't believe people are actually having sex and getting naked in front of each other!" The idea horrified me. I could not imagine opening myself up in that way to anyone, especially not someone who was only my boyfriend. I had also seen so many of my friends have sex only to have that person go have sex with another person. My friends came away from the experience deeply hurt. I listened to their stories and told myself that was not going to happen to me. I was already such a sensitive person; there was no way I'd allow myself to be hurt in that way. When the subject came up in my long talks with Kaelin, the two of us were always on the same page. We did not want to have sex with *anyone* any time soon.

KAELIN:

When I started to pursue Kyrah, I committed myself to respecting her and to getting to know her and to honoring her boundaries just like she respected mine. Neither of us wanted a relationship based on infatuation and hormones. From the start, we set out to lay the kind of foundation upon which a future marriage could be built. As Christians, we were committed to not having sex before marriage, but our commitment level went beyond that. The two of us talked a lot about having a dating relationship that honored God.

Our goals were a very good thing. However, I let my pride run rampant and came to the conclusion that our level of commitment put us on a higher level than the people I went to school with. I looked around at how low my classmates' expectations were for themselves, and I just knew I'd write a book one day to raise the standard. I planned to call the book *Worth the Wait* because of its primary message: I waited until marriage to have sex and so should you. What I didn't want to admit to myself was the fact that I wasn't quite as pure as I told myself I was. I had secrets I couldn't bring myself to tell anyone, secrets about both my past and habits I still struggled to break. That story will come later. For now, I was Kaelin the wise who knew all about building a relationship with a member of the opposite sex that was going to be so strong it would someday lead us to the altar.

KYRAH:

My school had a winter formal right after school started back up after Christmas break. Kaelin asked me to go to it with him, and my dad actually agreed to let him take me. Kaelin and I even coordinated what we were going to wear to the dance. I was so excited. I was going to get to show my guy off at my school. The two of us were going to have so much fun.

I started talking about the upcoming dance and Kaelin with one of my guy friends. He listened for a while; then he asked, "So is Kaelin your boyfriend?"

"No, I guess, not officially," I said.

"What do you mean not officially? You either are or you aren't…"

"Well, I mean, we're together and we're committed to each other and neither of us is seeing anyone else. He's met my parents. We have an understanding, I guess," I said.

"So, he's your boyfriend," my friend replied.

"He hasn't actually asked me to be his girlfriend. We've talked about it and we both agree that those labels don't mean anything, so why use them? Labels don't define who we are or what our relationship is all about," I said.

My friend looked at me with a smirk on his face. "Listen, Kyrah, I'm a guy and I know how guys think. He's obviously afraid of commitment and is just lying to you. Don't get too attached is all I'm saying."

"You don't know Kaelin," I said.

"Keep telling yourself that," he said.

My friend wasn't the only one with whom I had some variation of the exact same conversation. A lot of my friends told me they thought Kaelin had commitment issues. They gave me a hard time about it.

Even my mom got in on the act. Kaelin was over at my house one afternoon when my mom came out and asked him, "So what's the deal with you two? Are you her boyfriend or not? What am I supposed to say about the two of you when people ask?"

Kaelin smiled and went into his explanation of how we didn't need the labels of boyfriend and girlfriend to describe what our relationship was really about. My mom rolled her eyes, said something like, "Uh-huh. Sure," and went on with her day. I have to be honest. Even though I agreed with Kaelin about how we didn't need labels, my life would have been a lot easier if I could have simply called him my boyfriend instead of referring to him as my special friend whom I go out with and who took me to the winter formal and who I spent Valentine's Day with and who later asked me to go to prom. I always had to explain that we're committed to each other but that we don't call each other boyfriend and girlfriend because those labels don't define us. Kaelin just laughed it off. I think the more people pressed him about it, the more determined he was not to give in.

KAELIN:

I could tell Kyrah was getting annoyed by all the questions people asked her about us and having to defend me to her friends. They said I had commitment issues, but to me, I felt like we had an even greater commitment without the labels. I had my eye on a greater prize. I didn't have to repeat it, but from the start, I had told Kyrah I date to marry. To me, labels now didn't matter. If we became husband and wife, what did it matter whether we'd called each other boyfriend and girlfriend in high school?

But there was another side to how adamant I was about not using the same labels as everyone else, one not quite so noble. In my pride, I thought I was above all this high school nonsense, even though I was also in high school. I also enjoyed going against the flow, especially since the flow always seemed to go in the wrong direction. Remember, I was raised to be a leader, not a follower. I fight against any system that I don't believe in. Looking back, I regretfully admit that my battle against labels came out of my arrogance and insecurities as much as it did out of any convictions about having a Christ-honoring relationship. I went to the other extreme as a way of overcompensating for my own internal struggles. I didn't want to admit to my struggles. Instead, I wanted to project strength like a leader. Now I know real leaders aren't afraid to show weakness, and they don't overcompensate to convince people they're perfect.

My fight against labels lasted all the way up to October 18, 2014. I remember the day because Kyrah asked me to go to her family reunion. Every year, her extended family gets together, but this was the first time in a long time Kyrah's immediate family was attending. The reunion was a really big deal, and Kyrah wanted me to meet all of her grandparents and aunts and uncles. She took me over to a group of her aunts. "This is my friend Kaelin," Kyrah said. In Black families that's typically how new boyfriends get introduced. So far, so good.

"So, your boyfriend?" one of her aunts teased.

"Well, not exactly…," Kyrah replied. She gave me a look that said a lot more than her words.

Her aunts picked up on Kyrah's frustration and the interrogation began.

"What's your name? What school do you go to? What are your parents' names?" her aunts fired away. I couldn't even answer one question before another was asked.

"Do you have a job? Do you drive? Did you drive HERE? Did you drive HER HERE?" There were so many questions coming from so many directions there was no way I could answer them all. I figured they were testing me, and I needed to keep my composure and not fold. So I took all the heat from Kyrah's family that I deserved that night. After all, I was the *genius* who decided to show up to a *family reunion* before properly defining our relationship.

The pressure didn't end with the aunts. Kyrah's dad comes from a family of giants. Her uncles were some tough-looking guys. To my surprise, her uncles didn't have many questions. They seemed to know most guys my age were all talk, and frankly, guys like her uncles don't typically need to say much. I knew they meant business as they sized me up when I approached them to be introduced. Like I said, they didn't say much, but what I do clearly remember was a firm "Don't mess this up with her." I'm still here to write this, so I guess I'm doing fine so far.

Through all the interrogations and uncomfortable introductions, Kyrah's aunts and uncles kept coming back to the question of who I was if I wasn't Kyrah's boyfriend. For the first time, I finally understood Kyrah's frustration. It wasn't just the questions but also the looks her family gave me. I finally realized that no one really cared about my high-sounding ideals about doing things differently. Instead, I was only making Kyrah's life more complicated. I knew how to end that. Toward the end of the night, I pulled Kyrah aside and asked, "Will you be my girlfriend?"

"Yes," she simply said.

Just like that, we were official. I hadn't surrendered my convictions. Instead, I'd learned that often in a relationship you have to compromise to do what is best for the other person.

Everything was much simpler after we had a name for what we were. Although my intentions had been good, not properly defining the relationship had made things pretty complicated. When I finally got to see how my stand against the system had complicated Kyrah's life, I had to wonder why I'd waited so long. If the words boyfriend and girlfriend were nothing but labels that did not define who we were, why had I been so hesitant to use them? Perhaps I cared more about how people saw me than I had in junior high. This time I wasn't embarrassed about their disapproval about who I was dating, but about the perception of what I was doing in my relationship. I had a history that I wasn't proud of, and thankfully not many people knew it.

Yet, even though my past was largely secret, I still felt haunted and ashamed by it. Running from my past led to me overcompensating to prove I had really changed my ways. But I had to wonder how much I had really changed. Mentally I had made a commitment not to have sex until marriage, but physically I found it more difficult than ever to contain that fire. I was sixteen, and my hormones were firing on all cylinders. The struggle left me frustrated. I felt like I should be able to keep this fire under control, and I had an unconventional idea for that as well.

During our year of me refusing to give in to the labels of boyfriend and girlfriend, Kyrah and I made sure to honor each other by not taking things too far physically. I had promised to build our relationship on more than lust, and that was my way of proving it. At first, keeping that commitment was easy. Both of us were so busy that we hardly ever got to go out. Kyrah was on the cheer team, which meant not only did she cheer at all the football and basketball games, but she also had extra practice after school and cheer competitions on a lot of weekends. I was involved in all kinds of extracurriculars and track, which tied me up through the week, on top of working part-time at a local credit union. We went to church together every Sunday, either at my dad's church or at Kyrah's church, but that wasn't quite the same as a date. Outside of a few big events like the winter formal and prom in the spring, even if we'd wanted to push the envelope physically, we didn't have the time or opportunity. And I was really thankful for that.

However, the longer we were together, the more I wanted to hold Kyrah in my arms and kiss her. It was all I could think about. Nearly a year had gone by with no real physical contact. I'd had girlfriends before, but none since the spiritual rebirth I wrote about earlier. If you'd asked the old Kaelin if he could have gone a year without kissing, I'd have laughed and said you were crazy. In my mind I had shown my seriousness and had nothing else to prove. But I wasn't going to just lay a kiss on Kyrah out of the blue. I didn't know how she'd react. After all, we both went along with the idea of no kissing. I had no idea if she'd changed her mind, but I sure as heck had changed mine.

Finally, I got up the nerve to bring up the subject. We had a rare time out, just the two of us, when I said, "Kyrah, there's something I've been thinking about."

"What's that?" she asked.

"I...uh..." I couldn't get the words out. *What is the matter with me?* I yelled at myself. *It's not like I've never kissed a girl before. Why am I so nervous?* But I knew the answer. I was nervous because I'd never kissed *Kyrah* before. My feelings toward her were unlike any I'd ever felt before. I knew I was falling in love with her. This wasn't lust. This was more than just infatuation. This was real and it was pure and it was special and she was so innocent, and what if I ruined it by taking it too far? *I can't blow it. I can't mess this up. Maybe I should stick with what we're doing, which is nothing, but man, I have to kiss her.*

"What is it?" she asked.

"I just want you…" *Yup, no going back now.* "I really want to kiss you," I said, unsure of what she'd say back.

Kyrah smiled and my heart melted. "Then do it," she said softly.

She stood there, gazing at me, expecting me to do something. I was entranced by those brown eyes until I instinctively leaned in and our lips met and my world started spinning.

When I went home that night and walked into my house, my mom and dad and my sister and her boyfriend were all in our living room. They took one look at me and they were all like, "Whooooaaaaaaaaa!" like a scene out of an old TV show. I was like, "What?" My mom looked at me and said, "You don't even have to say anything. It's written all over your face." I guess smitten doesn't just wipe off.

KYRAH:

Our first kiss was sweet, but the second made me really uncomfortable. Kaelin and I had gone to grab something to eat and we were driving around when he took a left turn into a park that's not too far from either of our houses. It was still daylight, but we weren't there to go for a walk. Kaelin pulled onto the side of the street, turned off the motor, and leaned over to kiss me. So far, so good. We started kissing—pecking, really—but I could feel the transition into longer kisses, almost making out. I had never done this before, but I had the distinct feeling Kaelin had. My face grew hot and I felt myself sweating even though it was not warm in the car. Everything in me was screaming that this shouldn't happen. I leaned back a little and said, "Kaelin, I've never done this before."

He looked me in my eyes and said, "I'll teach you."

And teach me he did! Afterward I realized I had never really kissed a guy before, not like that. We didn't cross any lines or do anything we needed to feel guilty about later. At least I didn't think we had.

Another time, Kaelin and I went out for someone's birthday. The night went really well, and on the way back to my house, we ended up in the same park on the same street. This time, however, the sun was down. Rather than lean over and start kissing me, Kaelin got out, came around to my side, and opened my door for me. I got out of the car, put my arms around his neck, and we kissed. And we kissed. Our kisses grew more and more passionate, but this time I wasn't uncomfortable. We ended up moving around to the back of his car, where I sat down on the trunk lid. Kaelin pressed himself up tight against me, and my legs instinctively wrapped around him. Our hands were moving, and when his hand moved up my fully clothed thigh, I thought, *Wow, now I get it. I understand how my friends at school end up going all the way.* I know I wanted more. All the while I kept hearing something buzzing.

When we finally stopped kissing, I realized the buzzing came from my phone. My mom was blowing it up. Finally, I answered, a little out of breath but doing my best to sound normal. "Where are you?" my mom asked with the tone that told me I should have been home already.

"We're on our way," I said.

"Okay," she said in a way that told me she didn't really believe me.

The drive home was very uncomfortable. Kaelin and I didn't say much. I did feel a little guilty, but it was honestly exhilarating. Here we were, a few weeks past never kissing, with me being fully ready to give in to wherever our lust wanted to take us. They say you don't know what you are missing until you try it, and wow, is that ever true. When he touched my thigh, my entire body responded.

When we did talk again, Kaelin said, "We can't do that again."

"I totally agree," I said.

"I don't want to do anything that's going to ruin what we have," Kaelin said.

"I don't want that either," I said.

Afterward, however, I started replaying the event in my mind. Had we really gone too far? I mean, what did we actually do besides kiss? Was kissing really that big of a deal? Honestly, I didn't know. Now I know that for him, it wasn't what we were doing but where it could go in a hurry that was the problem. It's hard to take things in a relationship slow when you find yourself wanting to push boundaries.

And it felt to me that Kaelin had pushed the boundaries before. I'd asked him about past girlfriends a few times, and his answers seemed reserved. I'd never made out with anyone besides Kaelin. I could tell he had. *How far has he really gone?* I wondered if this was something we should talk about, but I trusted him enough that if he had some secrets he needed to share, he would. I had no reason to think otherwise.

KAELIN:

That night at the park scared me because I saw how all our convictions about purity came crumbling down in the heat of the moment. Or should I say my convictions, because I was the one who took the initiative and wanted to push the envelope. It was my hands moving, not hers. I'd been in similar situations before, but I thought that was just something the old Kaelin struggled with. I never expected I'd let myself run back there so easily. *Maybe I should talk to Kyrah about that*, I thought. But I convinced myself there was no need. This was a one-time situation. Now that I'd seen my own limits, I'd pull back. Telling Kyrah about something that happened with another girl would only make her worry, and it wasn't like I'd had sex before. I had not. I was a virgin—technically, at least.

7

Worth Staying Home For?

KAELIN:

When I was in first grade, my parents moved our family out of the inner city and across town. We left behind a run-down neighborhood with a high crime rate and struggling schools for a place with well-kept homes, a very low crime rate, and schools that excelled. At first, I hated both my new neighborhood and my new school. I went from looking like everyone else to being the only Black kid in class. Even though I'd worked hard at school before, I now found myself behind in every subject because of the systemic inequality between schools that serve Black and white communities. Catching up was difficult, but the smaller class sizes and improved facilities certainly made a difference. Unlike at my old school, I was actually encouraged to do well, to push myself to get the best grades possible, and to dream of a better future. Starting in junior high, teachers talked about us going to college, but it wasn't the stuff of dreams. College felt like a real expectation for every student.

In my old neighborhood, no one talked seriously about college. If the subject came up, the goal was to get an athletic scholarship. Older people in the neighborhood held up historically Black colleges as a great goal as well, especially Morehouse College in Atlanta. If you were a young Black man, that was THE place to go. Dr. King went there. Parents dreamed that maybe someday their kids could too.

But Atlanta was a long way away, and so was college. Most families in my old neighborhood felt blessed if their kids finished high school. A four-year university felt like a pipe dream except for someone lucky enough to land an athletic scholarship. That was the only way anyone believed they could pay for a college education. No one ever talked about going after academic scholarships. Even if you had the brains to try for one, you didn't because no one wanted to be the nerd. The more you excelled academically, the more you regressed socially. If you wanted to be cool and get the girls to like you, you had to be an athlete. Unfortunately, athletic scholarships are hard to land and even harder to keep after a life spent focusing on sports and not academics.

That was part of the reason why hardly anyone in the old neighborhood went to college. A few people still talked about it. College talk came up in the barbershop every time I went. "Back in my day I had a full ride," or, "Imma go back to school; I just have to…," but the talk rarely took anyone anywhere beyond inner-city Bakersfield. Everyone started out with big goals and big ambitions, but they never accomplished them because, at least in my old neighborhood, Bakersfield was the place where dreams go to die. If you got the chance to get out, you took it and you didn't look back.

A lot of people talked about grabbing their chance to get out, and a few actually had the opportunity, but the biggest thing that seemed to get in the way was getting "caught up"—that's what we called it. Getting caught up means two things. The first is letting a romantic relationship hold you back. Basically, that means letting your high school sweetheart keep you home. You get really caught up when you move on to the second meaning, which is having a baby with someone out of wedlock.

In our community, if a girl got pregnant, she had the baby, which put an end to all her dreams and plans for her future. The guy's life wasn't the same either, at least for the ones who chose or got the opportunity to stay with the mother. When the baby came, you had to find a job to support your new family. Once that happened, you didn't have the luxury of chasing any dreams. Instead, you stepped up and did what real men are supposed to do. That's what my dad did. That's what Kyrah's dad did. Other men conveniently got to decide fatherhood wasn't for them, only to leave the children they helped conceive fatherless. Before you throw shade on these guys, you need to realize you never really know what you will do if you find yourself in that spot. I believe these guys should take full personal responsibility and step up to be the father their child needs, but it's equally worth noting how the system isn't really set up for these guys to succeed.

Having grown up in that environment, I can see how people get caught up in it. It is hard to do better when you've never seen better. And after years of racism, discrimination, segregation, and brutality on full display, along with the stories of it being handed down and seeing it in the media, it is hard to believe you have a chance for a better life. I saw a lot of that in our old neighborhood because even though we left it, we didn't leave it. My dad's church was there, which meant we spent every Sunday and Wednesday immersed in that community.

Don't get me wrong, I love that community. It's *my* community. It's where I came from and the cloth that I'm cut from. I don't know many places with such down-to-earth people. While the people are great, it's the mind-set I had to escape, the mind-set that says there is no way out, the mind-set that says the life your parents had is the life you'll have…if you're lucky. That's what people call the "Bakersfield mind-set." Other communities across the country have different names for it. The same mind-set is everywhere.

My parents wanted more than that for my siblings and me, which is one of the reasons they moved to the other side of town. Moving into a more affluent neighborhood with better schools meant, by default, moving to a place that was more white. In my predominantly white high school, when my friends and I started talking about college, not going to a four-year university wasn't even a possibility. My siblings and I were the first generation in our family to entertain thoughts of going to a university. But at my high school, everyone went to college, as their parents had gone to college, and their grandparents before them, and on up the line.

Kids in my white high school also didn't seem to get caught up. They had sex as often as kids on the other side of town did, but pregnancy wasn't the life stopper and dream killer it was in my old neighborhood. If an unplanned pregnancy came along, people dealt with it and got on with life. At least that's how it looked to me. Or maybe the girls had better access to birth control on the more affluent side of town. Either way, the Bakersfield mind-set didn't seem to be a thing on this side of town.

My parents sacrificed to get us to this side of town with a different set of expectations, a different mind-set, a different view of the future. They wanted my siblings and me to have the opportunities to succeed they didn't have. While my parents didn't come out and say it in so many words, I knew I had to push myself and take advantage of every opportunity I had to move up in life and break the hold my hometown seemed to have.

That is why from the time I was in junior high I pushed myself to do well in school. During junior high and on into my freshman year of high school, I played football. I quit after my freshman year to focus on academics. College and beyond was my goal, and I couldn't let anything get in the way. I even picked my extracurricular activities with an eye toward making a good impression on future college admissions counselors.

KYRAH:

Being biracial, I also grew up in two worlds, but my experience was very different than Kaelin's. I struggled to find a place where I belonged, especially in junior high. I was too Black for the white girls and too white for the Black girls. Once I got to high school, I settled into a group of friends who accepted me the way I was, and life got better socially. Daja was one of the first friends I made in high school, and I instantly clicked with her. We were friends on and off through high school and ultimately ended up reconnecting in college and were inseparable. Any moment we weren't at school or with our boyfriends, we were with each other. Sometimes we would even ditch the boys to have a girls' trip to her grandparents' beach house over the weekend. She's truly one of the most selfless and kind people I've ever met. It has always been one of those friendships where we could go a year without talking and reconnect and it's like we never stopped talking. If you've ever met someone like that, you know those are the people you keep close because you don't come across them often.

Academics were a different story. I wasn't a bad student, just an unmotivated one. Unlike Kaelin, I wasn't bubbling over with major life goals I couldn't wait to chase. I needed someone to give me a gentle push at the right time or to water the seeds of possibility within me to get me going, but no one did. My parents did the best they could, but their relationship had deteriorated to the point where I think they were both on the verge of giving up. I could see the toll all of the fighting was taking on my mom, and I felt really bad for her. The last thing she needed was for me to add more stress to her life. Instead, I did my best to survive my home life until something better came along.

And survival is the best way to describe my academic life. I started to believe that something had to be wrong with me, that I wasn't smart enough to do anything valuable. I ended up pretty much just floating along, doing what I needed to do to pass but never really thinking about pushing myself to get ready for anything after graduation. Everyone in my high school pretty much assumed that everyone else was going to go on to college, but I didn't have anyone in my life pushing me in that direction. That didn't stop me from joining in when friends started talking about going to USC or UCLA or Stanford, or even one of the Cal State schools like Fresno State. When the conversation turned to me, I always said I was going to go to San Diego State. I threw that name out only because I spent a week on campus for cheer camp one summer. San Diego State wasn't my dream school because I didn't have a dream school. I had no idea what I wanted to do with my life. I had no huge aspirations to do anything or be anything. Back in high school, I told people I wanted to be a teacher or a marine biologist, and maybe I did, but it was more just something that I said because I couldn't think of anything else.

During my junior year, a counselor came into one of my classes and explained the process of getting into college. She told us which schools we could realistically think about based on our grades. That's the first time I thought that maybe I should have put a little more effort into school and extracurriculars. California has three levels of public colleges and universities. At the top is the University of California system, which is made up of schools like UCLA and UC Davis and UC Berkeley. They're the hardest to get into. Because of my grades, I knew I didn't stand a chance of being accepted by any of them. A notch below the UC system is the California State University system, which consists of all the four-year universities with "state" in their name, like Fresno State and San Diego State. Below state schools is the community college system. A lot of people did their first two years at a community college, then transferred to a UC or CSU school. You can save a lot of money doing this, but there was an unspoken understanding that community college is thirteenth grade. I really did not want to go down that road.

I couldn't do anything about my past grades, but I thought that if I at least didn't fail any of my classes, I could probably get into my hometown school, Cal State Bakersfield. For other people, CSUB was a fallback school in case they couldn't get into anywhere better. For me, it was really my only option. My dad even promised to pay for my schooling if I went there. That sounded good to me. However, I didn't know where that might leave Kaelin and me. I loved him and hoped we'd spend the rest of our lives together. He was really the only good thing in my life at this time. My parents argued constantly. Some days Kaelin picked me up for a date and I'd be hyperventilating from crying so hard. He was my rock and my escape. But I knew Kaelin had no interest in going to CSUB. From the beginning of our relationship, he'd talked about going to Pepperdine University, which sits near the beach in Malibu. Even though Malibu was only two hours away, I thought our relationship couldn't survive if he went there. Between the beach and all the girls he'd meet, there was no way he'd want to stay tied to a girl stuck in Bakersfield. He also visited nearly every college in the state of California—at least it felt like that to me. Then, when it came time to apply to schools, he also applied to Baylor and Texas Christian University, both of which are in Texas. We talked about why he did this. He told me that he wasn't going to stick around Bakersfield for me. He said it in a more diplomatic way than that, with lots of promises about how we'd make the long-distance thing work. "I don't want us both to stay in Bakersfield and miss out on getting the full college experience," I think is how he put it. I played it tough. "Don't think I'm going to stick around here just for you either," I said, even though I was dying inside. I didn't know what I'd do if he went away for college.

My going to college anywhere almost became a moot point. I failed a math class my senior year, which made me think I had blown my chance of getting in anywhere, even CSUB. I went home crying, embarrassed that I couldn't get into the school that literally everyone gets into. Even though I didn't have some grand plan for my life, I knew that going to any college opened doors to a better life. Neither of my parents went to college. My mom was a stay-at-home mom who poured her everything into her kids. However, staying home left her completely dependent on my dad. She used to tell me not to put myself in that position but to always have a way of making it on my own. How could I make it on my own if I didn't go beyond a high school education?

Thankfully, by some miracle from God, I received my acceptance letter to CSUB. I was going to be a Roadrunner. I didn't care that I was going to live at home and commute. That was fine with me. I was happy I got in.

KAELIN:

Even though I was in love with Kyrah, I was determined not to let my decision on where I went to college be influenced by our relationship. Through the Black student union at my high school, I visited a lot of different universities, but I only wanted to go to one place: Pepperdine. I'd become infatuated with it from watching a television show called *Zoey 101* as a kid. On television it had looked like the ultimate college experience, and that's what I wanted. When I visited the campus my sophomore year, I completely locked into it. I wanted to go to a Christian school and perhaps major in religion or something related to apologetics. Pepperdine checked that box. I come from a long line of entrepreneurs going back generations. My dad not only pastors a church; he started and owns his own heating and air-conditioning company. I wanted to follow in his footsteps by someday starting a business of my own. That's why wherever I went to school needed to also have a good business program. Again, Pepperdine checked that box. I thought about either going to law school or perhaps pursuing a master's degree or an MBA once I finished my undergraduate degree. With Pepperdine, I could go either route and stay where I was. To my young mind, Pepperdine felt like the perfect fit. When I checked out their entrance requirements and compared them to what I brought to the table, I knew I had a *really* good chance of being accepted. That settled it. It was Pepperdine or bust, baby. There was one little problem: how to pay for it. At that time, tuition and housing and all the fees came to around $65,000 per year.

I've never been one to back off from a challenge. The prospect of having to pay a quarter of a million dollars over the course of four years for my degree did not make me run. Instead, I started looking for a path to get to where I wanted to go. I had the grades to get some academic scholarships, but those are hard to come by in California. That left the old reliable standby from my old neighborhood: an athletic scholarship. I'd quit football my freshman year, not that it mattered with Pepperdine. Even if I had been good enough to get some attention as a football player, they didn't have a team. Basketball also was not an option. I can hoop, but I'm one of those "park all-stars." Real basketball players are on another level. I discovered Pepperdine had a tennis team, so I thought I should give that a try. After a friend took me out and wiped the court with me, I realized there wasn't enough time in the world for me to get good enough at tennis to play for my high school, much less make a college team.

I kept going through the list of sports played at Pepperdine, and none of them matched my skill set until I noticed track. I'm a pretty fast runner, but I saw my opportunity not as a runner but as a jumper. Long story short, I went out for my high school team, and by the start of my senior year, I had broken the existing records and was jumping well enough to get some serious looks from colleges. My plan was coming together.

Until it wasn't. I applied to Pepperdine and was accepted. I visited the campus again for an early new-student orientation. By what I thought was a sign from God, I saw the track coach on the field while I showed my parents around the school. I nervously walked over and got his attention. "Hey, Coach, I'm Kaelin Edwards. I reached out to you via email this past fall right after I applied here."

To my delight, the coach remembered me. "Yeah, Kaelin, good to finally meet in person," he said.

"You too," I said. "I'm here visiting because I got accepted and Pepperdine is my top school choice." From my research, I'd noticed that my high school marks were already better than those of the best jumpers in their conference, so I added, "I think I can be a great asset to the team, and if you offer me a scholarship, I'll sign today."

What I thought was going to be one of the best days of my life quickly turned into one of the worst. The coach explained to me that because of Title IX, which dictates colleges maintain a balance between men's and women's sports, he could only offer scholarships to runners, not jumpers. The school didn't even have a long jump pit. "However," he said, "if you want to walk on to the team, I'd love to have you. We don't have a jump pit here on campus, but there's one nearby at Malibu High School. I'm sorry I don't have any scholarship money to offer you, but if you want to come out for the track team, I can make it happen," he said.

My heart sank to my shoes. That wasn't the news I'd hoped to hear, and the coach could see it on my face. "Thanks, Coach," I said. "I'll let you know." As I walked away, both the coach and I knew that I'd never suit up for him.

Without a track scholarship, there was no way I could afford Pepperdine. But I couldn't accept that reality. I had to find a way to make my plan work. I qualified for enough federal grants and scholarships to cover half the cost of attendance. That left borrowing enough money to cover the other half as my only option. However, I could not borrow the full $30,000 a year in student loans. Then I discovered a thing called Parent PLUS Loans that could cover the rest. At first, my parents shot that idea down. "Why don't you go to Morehouse instead?" they asked. Although Morehouse offered more money in scholarships, Pepperdine was the more highly ranked school, especially for the programs that I wanted to go for. When they saw my disappointment, my parents softened slightly to the idea of taking out loans in their name. They agreed to do it on the condition that I pay them back in full.

The moment my parents agreed to take out the loans if I repaid them, I was elated. My dream of going to Pepperdine was going to come true. My friends thought I talked a lot about Pepperdine before, but they hadn't heard anything yet. I wore so much Pepperdine gear at school that people even started calling me Pepperdine. Nothing was going to stop me now!

And then I discovered a man named Dave Ramsey.

My high school econ teacher used some material by Dave Ramsey, but I didn't pay much attention to him. At the time, all I cared about was the business part of my econ class. But then one day I was driving home from my job at the credit union and I came across Dave Ramsey's radio show on a podcast app. On this particular day, Ramsey was talking about how debt is dumb and how avoidable student loans were the dumbest form of debt.

The more he talked, the more I listened. Ramsey struck a chord with me because he hated debt even more than my dad. And my dad hated owing anyone anything. People started calling in to the Ramsey show and spilling their dirty laundry about their bad financial decisions. Student loans topped most people's lists. That made me think.

I kept going back to the Dave Ramsey show. The longer I listened, the more I began to see my dream university, the school I'd planned to attend since I was in junior high, in a whole new light. Instead of the beautiful campus overlooking the Pacific Ocean, I saw six-figure debt and me trying to pay it with a degree in religion. The math didn't work. Nor did it work if I majored in business or went on to law school. Law school meant even more debt I now questioned taking on.

My dream started to die, but I didn't want to give up so easily. I started googling the schools my friends talked about attending and the cost of attendance at each one. A lot of the schools were nearly as expensive as Pepperdine. Yet many of these friends came from families who could afford to send their kids to the best—and most expensive—schools. That wasn't my family. My dad was a bi-vocational pastor, and I was one of six kids. He and my mom couldn't pay over $100,000 over four years to keep me out of debt. It was not fair of me to even ask them to.

After wrestling with the math for months, I realized my dream had to die. In the words of Dave Ramsey, it was time to act my wage. I called the admissions office at Pepperdine and said the words I never thought could come out of my mouth: "I appreciate the offer, but I am going to have to pass. I am going to go to school somewhere else."

Now the question was where. I had options because I'd applied to other schools through the Common App just in case I didn't get into Pepperdine. Morehouse College had accepted me and offered me some scholarship money, but it was just as expensive as Pepperdine and not as highly ranked. I crossed it off my list. I really liked Cal Poly in San Luis Obispo and TCU in Fort Worth, Texas, but rather than receiving acceptance letters, I was told I was on their wait list. "Many, if not most, of the students on the wait list get in," they told me, but cocky seventeen-year-old me didn't want to hear that. If they didn't want me the first time, I didn't want to go there. I crossed both off my list, which was now getting very, very short.

The Cal State campuses were an option, which opened up Fresno State and San Diego State and every other California University with "state" in its name. However, we had a Cal State campus close to home. Why pay to stay in a dorm in Fresno or San Diego for basically the same level of education I could get while living at home? That didn't make any more sense than going deeply into debt to go to my first choice.

With no other decent options, my college "choice" fell to the last place on earth I wanted to go to: Cal State Bakersfield. I thought of the school as a joke. I'd only applied there because we had to as an assignment in one of my high school classes. I didn't celebrate when they accepted me. Of course they accepted me. They accepted most people who applied. And I did not want to live at home and commute, but what choice did I have? With all the financial aid and scholarships I received, I was literally getting paid to go to CSUB if I lived at home.

All through junior high and high school, I'd dreamed of escaping my hometown and going away to college to start a new life. Now I had to face the cold reality that I wasn't going anywhere, not for a while, at least. I had told Kyrah that I was not going to get caught up, that I was not going to choose to stay in Bakersfield for her. As it turns out, she wasn't the reason I stayed in town, but I stayed. She was thrilled. I tried to act happy, but from the first day of class at CSUB, all I could think was that I did not belong here. I guess I shouldn't have been surprised that my first year didn't exactly go the way I had planned.

8

First Brush with Marriage

KYRAH:

I was perfectly content at Cal State Bakersfield, and Kaelin was perfectly miserable. Even though I commuted back and forth to school, I pretty much lived on campus. Between my classes and studying in the library and hanging out with friends in the student center, I never left.

Kaelin only showed up for classes when he absolutely had to, and then he left as quickly as possible.

I built some really strong friendships with people I met at school.

Kaelin didn't think he belonged at CSUB and didn't connect with anyone.

Even though I had to study more than I ever had in my life, my grades were pretty decent.

Kaelin rarely went to class, and his grades showed it.

For the first time ever, I felt like I had control over my own life. I loved that first taste of freedom college gave me. I spent less and less time at home and more and more time with my friends. In high school I'd been very dependent on my mom, but not anymore. I was finally starting to become my own person.

Kaelin felt trapped, like he was living out his worst nightmare. I think no matter how that first year went, he was going to be miserable. Every time he drove to campus, he was reminded that he wasn't where he wanted to be, where he thought he deserved to be.

For me, everything about college was new and exciting. I could have stayed at Cal State four years and been completely happy.

Kaelin couldn't get out of there fast enough. He wasn't the only person I knew who was miserable at Cal State Bakersfield. For a lot of people, CSUB was the fallback school, the safe place close to home where you went if you didn't get accepted to, or couldn't afford, any of your first choices. Hardly anyone went there because they wanted to be there. And almost everyone commuted, which made it feel like a step above community college. I think that played a huge part in the low morale on campus.

I was very content there, although, honestly, I think I could have been just as happy anywhere. I have this habit of choosing the path of least resistance, and going to college in my hometown and living at home definitely was the easiest path I could have taken. My dad had offered to pay for at least my first year, along with a car and my books and gas. That had made the choice simple for me.

CSUB might have been an easy choice, but I went all in with it. I tried out for and made the spirit squad. Then, once classes started, I met a lot of people who, like me, were the first in their family to go to college. That bond created friendships because we all felt like we were in this together. We studied together and hung out together. I even reconnected with Daja. I mentioned earlier that we were friends throughout high school, but junior and senior year we really lost touch. We now bonded over both of us having super strict parents and experiencing our newfound freedom in college. Our times together at her grandparents' beach house in Pismo are still some of my favorite memories from that time of my life, and I'm so thankful I had a friend to enjoy life with.

Between classes and studying and hanging out with friends and the spirit squad, I didn't have much time for Kaelin and me. When we were together, he didn't hide how miserable he was. "How can you be so content at such a boring school?" he asked.

"I don't think it's boring. I like it here," I said.

He shook his head and said, "I don't get it." Nothing I said made him feel any better, so I stopped trying. It was like the two of us had traded places. Back in high school, he was on the debate team and ran track and was actively involved in his school. He studied like crazy and got good grades and was really into the whole experience. On the other hand, I pretty much slid by in high school, doing the absolute bare minimum. Now I was the one who was living my best life, and he was sliding by. I really didn't see how he was going to stick it out for the next four years, or how I could help him cope.

KAELIN:

The day I registered for classes at CSUB, I tried to convince myself I'd made the right decision by choosing to go there. *This is the place I can afford*, I told myself. *Better to be here for four years than be in debt for twenty to go to Pepperdine. Besides, maybe it won't be so bad here after all. Since this place is barely a step above high school, classes will be a breeze. I'll ace everything, have a killer GPA, and waltz into any law school I choose.*

Then I had another epiphany. Since classes were going to be a cakewalk, I could load up my schedule and finish in two and a half years, tops. On top of that, easy classes would leave me all kinds of time for extracurricular activities. Back in high school, I was the top triple jumper in the Central Valley of California. When the CSUB track coach heard that, she invited me to join the team. How could I say no? CSUB may not have been a great school, but at least its sports teams competed at the highest level, NCAA Division I. Coach loaded me up with all the CSUB athletic gear that came with being a D-I athlete, which made me feel like I was THE man on campus.

The Bible says that pride comes before the fall (see Proverbs 16:18), and my fall came fast. I walked onto campus thinking I was better than this place, so imagine the embarrassment I felt when people I knew from high school started looking at me funny when they saw me in class rocking my CSUB track team gear. "Why are you *here*? I thought you were going to Pepperdine," they asked time and time again. Immediately, I went on the defensive.

"I'm here because I didn't want to go four hundred grand in debt," became my standard answer. The more I had to answer these kinds of questions, the more trouble I had convincing myself there was any positive spin on being stuck in this place.

My plan to knock out my undergrad degree in two years also hit a wall. When I sat down with my academic advisor for the first time, he informed me that the university had a road map for every student. "Freshmen cannot declare a major," he said, "and we limit all freshmen to twelve units per quarter their first year. We find limiting your first year eases the transition from high school to college and sets you up to succeed in the long term."

"But I want to take twenty-one units," I said. I needed twenty-one to finish in two years.

"No freshman has ever taken twenty-one units," he replied.

I wanted to say, *But I'm not like any other freshman you've ever had here.* Instead, I asked, "So what do I need to do to take more?"

"There are no exceptions," he told me. "Every incoming student takes basically the same classes, which are the general core needed for every degree program."

I started to argue the point, but I realized it was a waste of time. Instead, I took the list of required classes and went out to make my schedule. My frustration only grew when I looked over my choices. I went down the list, class by class, and said, "Took it. Had it. Did it. WOW. I took every one of these 'required' classes as an AP class in high school! I can't believe they're trying to make me take them again."

I wouldn't have had to take them again to receive credit if I'd taken the AP tests after finishing the classes in high school, but I never did. I had to pay for the tests myself and didn't want to spend the money. I also didn't want a possible mediocre AP test score messing up my college transcript. Not taking the tests was my way of trying to finesse the system. I planned to artificially inflate my GPA by taking all honors and AP classes to impress college admissions counselors with my challenging schedule, thereby increasing the chances that I could get into any school I wanted. My plan didn't work out so great. Now I believed my grades in AP classes should have been enough to get college credit even without taking the AP tests. They weren't. I thought maybe there was a test I could take to test out of the classes…There wasn't. The only option was to retake my junior and senior years of high school. Classes hadn't even started and this school was proving to be a massive waste of my time.

By the time classes actually began, my attitude could not have been any worse. I kept working at the credit union where I'd worked throughout high school. *How hard could it be to balance work, school, and track?* I thought.

The answer was: very hard.

Track was the first casualty. College track was nothing like high school. We practiced on the track for a couple of hours every day, then hit the weight room. Then came the ice baths, mandatory tutoring, and event appearances, after which I had to sprint off to class or to work. A few weeks of this and I was burnt out. I started questioning why I was even putting myself through the trouble of trying to be a D-I athlete. It wasn't like I planned to jump in the Olympics. I only did track in high school to try to get an athletic scholarship from Pepperdine. That plan got me nowhere.

So why was I running track now? I made an appointment with the coach, apologized for wasting her time, and ended my collegiate athletic career before it even got started. All my life, I'd prided myself on never quitting anything I'd committed to. I broke that rule within my first month of college. I quit more things in those weeks than I had ever quit in my entire life.

My attitude only went downhill from there. I sat through my first couple of days of classes and came away more convinced than ever that they were a complete joke. Every lecture literally repeated the same material I'd learned in high school. After the first week, I didn't see much point in listening to lectures that I'd heard before. So I stopped going to class. I only showed up for tests, which I thought was more than enough to blow through these classes. As it turned out, my classes were a joke, but the joke was on me. I waltzed into my statistics class for my first test after not attending lectures and not even buying the book. When I got my test back with a big D+ on the top, I realized I probably needed to take this class a little more seriously.

But I didn't. Instead, I became even more discontent and more disconnected.

CSUB was on a quarter system. At the end of my first quarter, my GPA was a whopping 0.67 on the four-point scale. 0.67! On that scale, 1.0 equals a D average, and I couldn't even hit that. I didn't know a GPA that low was even possible. As it turned out, all those classes I felt like I'd already taken, I hadn't. Of course the first couple of weeks of lectures sounded familiar. That was by design. The professors started us off slowly by reviewing material most of us should have already had. I quit going to class right before they began presenting the new material I needed to pass the classes. I also ended up missing several tests altogether.

My stellar GPA should have gotten me kicked out of school. The university put me on academic probation instead. As twisted as it may sound, instead of being thankful for a second chance, I thought the fact that they'd give a second chance to someone with such a horrible GPA was one more sign that CSUB wasn't a real college. I didn't even take full responsibility for my horrible grades. I chalked them up to my discontent. I knew I was much better than my GPA. I was simply in the wrong place to prove it. *I've got to get out of here before this place kills me*, I convinced myself. My first thought was to try to transfer to Pepperdine or Morehouse the following spring since they had already accepted me. However, neither school had magically become affordable. That left me scrambling for a plan B.

I researched the best and least expensive law schools in the country. The search led me to the University of Texas at Austin. I couldn't afford their out-of-state tuition any more than I could afford Pepperdine. *But what if I didn't have to pay out-of-state tuition*, I wondered. I dug a little deeper into the residency requirements for in-state tuition, not just for the law school but also for the university. I found all I had to do was live in Texas for a year and I qualified.

A plan started to hatch in my mind. I researched UT's business school. It was one of the best in the Southwest. That worked for me. They didn't have a strong religion department, but I had dropped the idea of majoring in religion after I'd turned down Pepperdine. The more I read about UT, the more convinced I became that this was THE place I needed to be. The UT Longhorns had always been one of my favorite college football teams, which made all of this feel like a sign from God pointing east toward Austin.

However, I didn't want to move permanently to the other side of the country without Kyrah. I know I once told her that I was not going to stay in Bakersfield just for her, but the truth was I could not imagine living anywhere without her. I loved her and wanted to spend the rest of my life with her. That meant I could either give up on moving to Texas or...Another idea popped in my head: Kyrah had declared as a nursing major, which was the only major a freshman could declare. UT had a top-notch nursing program as well, one that put CSUB to shame. *Surely she'd rather go to the best school possible*, I thought. *Maybe I can convince her to move with me.*

Now, I would never ask Kyrah to move across the country as my girlfriend. The two of us had been together for a couple of years now. From the start, I'd talked about dating to marry. We now constantly talked about getting married someday. *Why can't "someday" be now?* The two of us could elope, move to Texas, establish residency, work for a year to save money for school, then enroll at UT! I had enough money saved to get us there and pay for an apartment long enough for us to find jobs. And finding jobs should not be a problem because, from everything I'd read, jobs were everywhere in Austin. The more I thought about the plan, the more perfect it seemed. Not only could we start our life together, but we'd also get away from this joke of a university and get out of Bakersfield and within five years or so we'd be out of school and ready to start chasing our dreams for our lives.

I did more research into the greater Austin area. I could not see a downside. Austin looked like a great place to live. UT was an excellent school. And, in my mind, Kyrah and I were ready to be married. We weren't just in love with each other. I believed our relationship had a depth beyond its years. Over the past two years, we'd talked and talked and talked about everything under the sun. We didn't have any secrets—at least none I felt I needed to reveal to her. We communicated so well that I thought we were already a solid team. Taking the next step and getting married almost seemed like a formality, aside from the added *benefits* we could then enjoy.

All that was left was telling Kyrah my plan. If I knew her like I thought I did, she'd be all for it. The sooner we got started, the better.

KYRAH:

Kaelin met me in the library to study one afternoon. From the look on his face, I knew he had something on his mind other than studying. "I've found a way for both of us to go to a much better school, and it's going to be a lot cheaper than here," he said.

"Us?" I asked.

"Yeah, us. You and me. I don't want to move to Texas without you," he said.

"Texas?"

"Yeah. Austin, Texas, and the University of Texas. In-state tuition is dirt cheap in Texas. All we have to do is move there and live there long enough to establish residency, and we pay the in-state rate. We'd just have to elope first," he said in a very matter-of-fact tone.

My heart skipped a beat. "Elope?" I said, trying to keep my voice from jumping too much with excitement.

"Well, yeah. We couldn't move there together without getting married first," he said.

It wasn't exactly a proposal, but the moment he mentioned getting married, I was on board. I loved him so much and we'd talked about marriage so often the conversation was not embarrassing or new to me. "You want to elope?" I asked, barely hiding my excitement.

"Absolutely," he said. "We both know we're going to get married someday. Now is as good a time as any."

"Wow. Okay. That's a lot to think about," I said, nearly in shock. We'd taken everything so slow through our entire relationship that I could not wrap my head around taking such a huge step so fast. I didn't know if the timing was right or not, but Kaelin is such a major planner that I trusted his wisdom. He literally doesn't do anything without planning out every detail beyond what anyone else might do. Most of his plans ended up in a notebook he'd carried around since long before we started dating. Any time he wanted to talk about the future, the notebook came out. The conversations often left me feeling inadequate because Kaelin had such clearly defined goals for his life and I had none. However, this time around, these life plans were about both of us. I felt like a partner in the discussion, not an uncomfortable observer. Kaelin genuinely wanted to know what I thought, which I appreciated.

"Honestly, what do we have to lose?" Kaelin added with a laugh. "We're young and this could be a pretty cool adventure and start to our marriage story. If it doesn't work out, we can always move back here. Our families won't let us starve."

I thought about what he said for a moment. College had given me my first taste of the freedom to make up my own mind. Maybe this was the next step. "I mean, I think we should at least look into it more," I said. "I never imagined living in Texas."

Over the next few weeks, we hardly talked about anything else. Most of our talks came late at night. We'd talk and talk, and by the time I went to sleep, I'd know I was about to be a married woman on my way to Austin. But the next morning, I'd wake up and wonder why I thought it was a good idea. With living at home and going to CSUB, life was pretty good. All my needs were taken care of. I had built some close friendships. I was on track to be the first person in my family to actually finish college. Did I really want to throw all this away to go struggle in some little Texas apartment fifteen hundred miles away from everyone and everything I loved?

I might have made it past that argument, but then I thought about what our eloping might do to the rest of our family. Eloping is supposed to be sudden and secretive, but Kaelin and I both discussed our possible plan with our families. To my surprise, my parents didn't hate it. However, my mom wasn't feeling the idea of Kaelin and me getting married in front of a judge. Honestly, I don't know how much she was feeling the idea of me marrying Kaelin, period. It seemed that the closer Kaelin and I grew to each other, the more tension grew between my mom and me. She'd liked him the first time she met him, but lately she started finding fault with everything he did. "He's too controlling," she'd say, or, "You need to date more than one person in your life. Don't settle for your first serious boyfriend." Every time Kaelin came over to our house, you could feel the tension in the air. As my parents' marriage got worse, I felt like my mom projected a lot of her frustration with my dad onto Kaelin. "All men are alike. Don't trust them," she'd told me before.

However, when I first mentioned eloping, she didn't go to any of her earlier arguments against him. Instead, she said, "You've always dreamed of a big wedding. I don't want to see you have that taken away from you."

"Maybe when I was little, but that doesn't matter to me now," I said.

"Oh, Kyrah. Every girl dreams about the perfect wedding. If you just go to a judge, you'll end up regretting it for the rest of your life."

"I don't know, Mom," I said. "I really just want to be married to Kaelin."

"That's okay, but you need to do it right," my mom countered. "Your aunts and uncles will be so upset if they don't get to watch you get married. I get upset just thinking about it."

We kept having this same conversation over and over for days and days until I finally gave in. "Okay, Mom. I won't get married in front of a judge," I said. She'd worn me down and I hated conflict so much that I found it easier to let her have her way than to keep arguing the point with her. This wasn't the first time my mom had worn me down to get her way. I had not yet learned how to stand up to her. I didn't realize this was her way of manipulating me, and I went along and let her do it, even when it came to my own wedding day!

The next time Kaelin and I discussed the Texas elopement plan, I brought up the wedding. "We can't go to a courthouse and not have our families there," I said. That led to a discussion about what it might cost to do a wedding ceremony. He had starting pricing engagement and wedding rings and thought he'd be able to find something for a few hundred dollars. I laughed then and I laugh even more now because rings aren't cheap, but

Kaelin was trying to juggle having enough money for a ring and a honeymoon and a life in Texas afterward. The latter was going to be a lot more expensive than either of us had ever believed, between the cost of insurance and tuition and food and rent and everything else we were going to need.

Kaelin's plan unraveled pretty quickly after that. Together we decided that it wasn't realistic. We knew the first year of marriage can be tough in general, and we didn't want to add the stress of money on top of that. Our change of plans didn't close the door on marriage in the future. Far from it. For me, not eloping and moving to Texas was a win-win. I got to stay at school and keep the life I was perfectly content living. On top of that, I knew it was now only a question of when, not if, Kaelin was going to propose. I didn't know if he'd wait until after we finished college, but I knew he was going to ask me to marry him. Eventually. I hoped. I soon learned I shouldn't have been so confident.

9

The Dawn of Kaelin and Kyrah

KAELIN:

The day after I officially gave up the dream of eloping with Kyrah and moving to Texas, I went back to class just as I did every day and afterward headed off to the credit union where I'd worked as a teller since my junior year of high school. Most days we weren't very busy at work, which gave me a lot of time to think. Maybe too much time. *So, what now?* I thought as I sat waiting for a customer to come in the door. *What now?*

After my first-quarter disaster, I retook the classes I'd failed and was back in good standing at school. I was finally able to make progress and start taking some business classes. I'd settled on accounting as a major. My boss at the credit union told me that with an accounting degree I could keep working there as long as I wanted and start moving my way up the corporate ladder. But I didn't choose to major in accounting so that I could work for someone else for the rest of my life. I really admired the freedom my dad had being a business owner. He always taught us that instead of working for the man, we could be the man and start our own business. He'd done that when he started his own HVAC company. I even worked some jobs with him when I was a freshman in high school. In true Edwards male fashion, I secretly wrote up a business plan and dreamed I'd take over the company so that my dad could devote all his time to ministry. My dad wasn't exactly eager to turn his company over to a fifteen-year-old, but he encouraged me to keep dreaming big. "You got entrepreneurship in yo' blood, just like me and my dad," he told me.

My dad didn't have to tell me this for me to know it was true. For as long as I can remember, I've always hatched plans to start some little business to make some money. Some of the plans weren't so little. As a kid, I sold candy at church and around the neighborhood, but by the time I was a freshman in high school, I was running my first semi-successful ventures. I decided to start a custom video game controller company. I would buy the controllers, both new and used, cheap on eBay. I then took the controllers apart, changed out the buttons, spray-painted them, and sold them as custom units. Sales jumped so big and so fast I had to hire six people to keep up with orders. Unfortunately, I made a classic rookie mistake by pricing everything too low to make a consistent profit. The business ended up going under when a flood of international orders came in and I had not charged enough to cover the extra cost of shipping out of the country.

I thought about my video game controller business as I sat at my teller's window with nothing else to do. *I came so close to making it*, I thought. *And it was so much fun while it lasted.* I had worked a ton of hours trying to make the business successful, but it hadn't seemed that much like work. Since then, I'd always had some sort of side hustle going, just to feed my creative juices. Even while working at the credit union, I did web design and marketing for some churches and small businesses. By now, I was making as much on my side hustle as I did at my regular job. *So why am I working here?* I wondered. *What do I really want to do?*

I enjoyed web design, but I didn't know if I had a real passion for it or if my joy came from running a business. *If not web design, then what?* One word popped into my head: *YouTube.* My brother Kevin started on YouTube in 2006 with some comedy and parody videos. A bunch of them went viral. He actually started making money with it in December 2007, when YouTube first launched its Partner Program. That led me to create my first channel, a gaming channel, in 2009. Unlike my brother, I didn't make any money off my channel because back then you couldn't monetize gaming channels because of copyright concerns around recording the games. That's what led me to starting and failing at my controller company. I had to figure out how to make money somehow. Two years later, I stopped making controllers and gaming videos. I found it hard to stay motivated without some sort of payoff in the end. Then in 2014, at the beginning of my senior year of high school, I started a vlog channel I called *Life with Kaelin. With* was the key word. I envisioned the channel growing into a community of people with similar goals and mind-sets, pushing one another as we navigated our way through the same stages of life. I designed the content not only to entertain but also to spark conversations. We'd encourage one another, challenge one another, grow with one another. Channels like this never go viral with millions of subscribers, but that was never my goal for my personal channel. I hoped to build a tribe with a goal to grow in all directions.

The more I thought about the channel, the more I wondered if I might be able to build something more. My brother had found success with his YouTube channels and was making good money through them. Sitting in my teller's window, day after day, bored, I wondered whether, if I devoted as much time and energy into my YouTube channel as I did my job, I could make it work too.

The more I thought about it, the more I wanted to go for it. But I couldn't dive in without a plan. This was about more than creating content for YouTube again—it was about starting a robust business behind the channel from scratch. If I was going to do it, I wanted to do it right. I began devouring every entrepreneurship and business book I could find. One Friday I stayed up most of the night reading, making notes, and contemplating what it was going to take to make it work. Finally, around five I drifted off. I was so locked in, I kept planning and strategizing while asleep. I never truly *rested* that night. When my alarm went off a little before seven for me to get up to go to work at the credit union, I could not move. The weight of the decision I knew I needed to make pinned me to the bed. Eventually I managed to roll out of bed to get halfway dressed, but I just couldn't finish. I was so anxious I could barely breathe as my throat began to tighten. *What's wrong with me?* I thought. I didn't even know, but my body did and had to make me physically ill so I would listen to it. I finally gave up and went back to hide in bed. The experience surprised me. I am always so confident and decisive, at least on the outside, but the combination of feeling stuck in place at a dead-end job, at school, and in life, along with the fear of not having a way out, put me into a panic attack that lasted all weekend. I didn't call in to work. Instead, I simply did not show up. I knew that meant "automatic termination," aka getting fired, but I did not care.

By Monday my panic gave way to resolve. I walked into work after going to class knowing what I had to do. My co-workers looked at me coming through the door and their eyes said, "Ooooo, Kaelin, you're going to get it now." I just smiled and kept walking. I clocked in and started my shift.

About halfway through my shift, my manager called me into her office. "Kaelin, you were a no-call and no-show on Saturday. You know that's grounds for an automatic termination, right?"

"Yes, I know. I'm sorry I didn't call in, but I couldn't. I had a panic attack at the idea of coming in Saturday morning and I just couldn't move."

"You had a panic attack over coming to work?" she asked.

"Yes. I'm spent. I just can't work here anymore," I said.

She looked shocked. "Why is that?" she asked.

"Working here is killing me inside. I've never been so depressed and anxious. I can't take it anymore. I'm fed up. On top of that, the work schedule I have now conflicts with my classes," I said.

"I'm surprised to hear that. This is a great job to have while you're in school, and we do our best to work around your schedule. I had even decided not to fire you over Saturday but to write you up instead to give you another chance," she said.

"I didn't come to go back and forth. It's nothing against you or anyone else here. This situation is not healthy for me, so today is my last day," I said.

"No two-week notice?"

"I'm sorry, this is it."

"If you don't mind me asking, what are you going to do instead?"

"I'm going to go all in with my online business," I said.

My manager kind of shook her head and handed me a piece of paper on which to write out my official resignation letter for her records. I wrote the statement, dated it, signed the bottom, and slid it across the desk to her. She picked it up, scanned it for a moment, then said something that I will never, ever forget: "Good luck with your little internet business." Nothing spurs on a true entrepreneur like having someone doubt they can make it. At least it did for me.

Over the next six months, I worked my channel like a full-time job. *Life with Kaelin* grew to about a thousand people who watched every week, eventually peaking at two thousand subscribers. However, no matter how much I worked the channel, I couldn't seem to grow it beyond the base of viewers I had. That sent me back to the drawing board.

I started researching how the largest YouTube channels grew an audience. I looked across all genres and learned quickly that the best of the best did what was trending at any given time. I decided I would do the same but with a unique twist that would let me stand out. I found lots of vloggers out there, but very few were Black, and even fewer had a consistent, positive, Christian perspective that was also fun. I started brainstorming what I could do in that space and writing my ideas in a notebook I'd carried with me since my freshman year of high school. I already had a channel that chronicled the journey from high school to college from the perspective of a young Black man. My channel felt very personal because I was inviting people into my life. I felt like I had more than subscribers—I had an online community.

However, something was still lacking. The more I looked at what others had done, the more I realized I needed two perspectives. If I was going to chronicle this life journey on into marriage, I'd need to have my future wife's perspective as well. I wasn't married, but I did have this serious girlfriend who I'd already tried to talk into eloping and moving off to Texas. Kyrah already appeared in some of my vlogs when she was with me. But as I researched what I needed to take my channel to the next level, I realized I needed Kyrah as a partner for her unique female perspective. Not only might this new perspective expand the audience to women, but I thought we'd also reach other young people interested in successful dating relationships. She didn't even have to be tied down to working with me. If this took off, she could do her own channel with her own insights into life.

Over the course of several weeks, I kept tweaking my plan. The more I worked on it, the more excited I became. I knew I needed to share it with Kyrah. I could not wait to see her reaction.

KYRAH:

"Hey, wanna grab lunch?" Kaelin texted me one day.

"Yes! :)" I immediately texted back. We hadn't seen much of each other in a few days. Between classes and work, we didn't get to hang out as much as either of us wanted. As soon as my class ended, I jumped in my car and headed over to our favorite chicken strip spot. I couldn't wait to see him.

When we sat down, I immediately wished I'd told him I had to study. Kaelin reached into his bag and pulled out the notebook he'd carried around as long as I had known him. This was Kaelin's planning notebook, his idea dump notebook, the place where he made plans for his life. Since our relationship had started getting more serious, those plans now included me. I was glad they did, but I hated the interrogation that often came with these conversations. "I've been thinking," Kaelin said.

My heart sank. "Really," I said with a tone of voice that, if he'd actually been listening, would have told him I did not want to have another notebook conversation.

"Yeah, I've been thinking about our future and what I'd like for us to do next and…" Kaelin started talking and talking and talking. It's like he was so excited he couldn't get the words out fast enough. As he talked, he opened his notebook to a page where he'd drawn three columns. At the top of the first, he'd written his name. At the top of the center column, he'd written "Kaelin and Kyrah," and at the top of the last column, he'd written my name. I couldn't quite make out what he had written under each one, but I knew he was about to tell me.

"…so the two of us, we need to have some mutual goals and a plan for how we're going to get there. Work takes up so much of our time and interferes with school and with our time together…," he went on. I sat there, quietly nodding my head, trying to look interested, but I knew where this was going. This was about us and our future, but not our future as a couple. No, this was about our future in business.

"How cool would it be if you got to make your own schedule and make money doing something that you are passionate about?" he went on. Kaelin spoke with so much passion and he wanted me to be just as passionate, but when he started talking about me tapping into what I was most passionate about, I was ready for the conversation to end. We'd talked about this before, and I never had anything to say.

"...and we could then create unique content for social media that would document our journey of transitioning from high school to college and then on to marriage and starting a family. As a woman, you can offer a completely different perspective that will resonate with a large part of the audience. So, what do you think you can do on the internet with what you are into?" he asked, and then stopped talking.

I didn't know what to say in response. So that's what I said. Nothing. Not one word. Knowing Kaelin the way I did, I knew he'd spent days working out all these plans in his notebook, probably not getting any sleep. Now he expected me to be all on board and have my own ideas with zero time to think about it. I couldn't do that. Unlike him, I didn't have tons of dreams for my life. I started off as a nursing major and later changed that to education, but it wasn't like I felt particularly passionate about either. I didn't feel much passion about anything. I knew that had to be weird, and that's how I felt right now with Kaelin looking at me, waiting for me to say something. He asked what I was into that I could share with an audience on YouTube, but I didn't have an answer because I didn't know. *How could I know so little about myself and Kaelin know so much about himself?* I wondered. He had so many dreams for the future. I was here for the chicken strips and to hang out.

It wasn't like this was the first time we'd had a serious talk about our futures. Our whole relationship started with the serious conversation where Kaelin told me he dated to marry. As long as I'd known him, he'd talked about all his big plans for the future. In those conversations he'd always asked about mine. I talked about college and working after that and getting married someday and having a family. My plans were always pretty vague, which had never been a big deal before. They had to be vague because I didn't really know where I wanted to be in five or ten or twenty years. I basically just took life as it came. I had no dreams I hoped to fulfill, so I never made any huge plans to reach them. Before, every time Kaelin and I had talked about the future, I'd never thought this was a big deal. And then he took out the notebook…By the time the conversation ended, I was nearly in tears, not so much because of anything Kaelin had done but because of my own frustration for knowing so little about myself.

KAELIN:

When Kyrah didn't immediately respond, I thought I just needed to give her some time. So, I sat there, waiting, silent. Five minutes went by. I thought, *Maybe I wasn't clear. Surely if she understood me, she would be as excited as I am.* When I couldn't take it anymore, I filled the awkward silence by rehashing what I'd already said. Surely now she'd have something to say, so I waited. Another five minutes of silence passed. I started to wonder if she was going to say anything. I really wanted to know what she thought. To me, the plan looked great. The two of us could work together and set our own hours and have so much more time together than we did now. So I waited another five minutes.

Finally, I realized that Kyrah's silent treatment was her answer. So, I changed the subject. I was pretty disappointed. My whole plan was about a lot more than expanding an online business through a YouTube channel. I thought that by doing this channel together, we'd get to set our own hours and have as much time as we wanted together, something we'd never really had.

I also did not want my plan to come across as mine alone. I went into the lunch hoping to pick her brain and for her to come up with what she wanted to share on the internet. If we did this together, which was the plan, it needed to belong to both of us. I wanted her to buy into the idea, to take ownership and run with it.

Unfortunately, after changing the subject away from my big idea, I went back to it. Instead of waiting for Kyrah to have ideas of her own and accepting her silence as an actual response, I said something like, "Well, I know you like makeup. So that's something you could talk about on YouTube." While I talked, I wrote down "makeup" in the column under her name. She did not say anything. I kept on naming things I thought she was into and writing them down. All I did was make an uncomfortable situation even worse. If Kyrah was ever going to come on board, it would have to be on her time, but I thought I could coach her through it and speed things up. Here's a tip for all you guys in relationships out there reading this book: Never, ever decide you can speak for your significant other. All you do is rob them of their voice, and I did not yet realize how Kyrah already struggled to find hers. I wish I could say I never made that mistake again.

After our awkward lunch, I didn't bring up Kyrah joining me on You-Tube for a while. I continued creating content alone on *Life with Kaelin*. Because I vlogged my life, the people in my life turned up on camera pretty often, including Kyrah. My community loved her being in my videos. More and more people started asking about our relationship. Then she got a new job, which took more of her time and naturally kept her off camera since we hung out less. The comment section lit up with the same question: Where is Kyrah? I reminded my audience that this channel was called *Life with Kaelin*, but they kept asking, "Where is Kyrah?" I started to wonder if anyone actually tuned in to see me.

KYRAH:

I was happy for Kaelin that he kept doing his channel without me. The last thing I wanted to do was hold him back from chasing his dream. However, the whole experience showed me how completely different Kaelin and I are from each other. The conversation over lunch made it feel like he was trying to force me to grow into someone he wanted me to be. There was a time in my life when I would have gone along with it, but I didn't want to do that now. For the first time in my life, I had a level of freedom, with my own car and a group of friends at school. Eventually I knew I'd have to take the next step after graduating from college, but that was still nearly three years away and I was in no hurry to get there. I think that's part of why I reacted the way I did to Kaelin's idea of launching our own YouTube channel. Not only did I feel like I had nothing to share with the world, but I also saw no need to make a huge change to a life I enjoyed.

One of the things I've always admired about Kaelin is his work ethic. When he does something, he goes all in, and that's how he approached his YouTube channel. If he wasn't filming, he was editing a video or uploading new content to his channel. The two of us talked about his channel all the time. He constantly bounced ideas off me for changes he was thinking about making. I liked that. He truly did value my opinion.

When Kaelin first launched his channel, I did my best to stay off camera, but as time went on, I started to warm to the idea of being on camera. I didn't have to share my opinions or try to make any kind of profound statement. I was just myself. After a while, it was like the camera disappeared and we just did our life together.

My camera time changed when I had to start working more hours. My dad had promised to cover all my expenses for my first year, but after the first year, I had to start paying for my own tuition, gas, books, and things like that. I didn't see that as a big deal. At least I had a year to adjust to college life. However, when I started working more, I wasn't able to appear on Kaelin's channel as much as I had before. Again, I didn't see that as a big deal since it was his channel. But it was. Kaelin came to me and asked if I'd be willing to do YouTube with him full-time. This time I felt more open to it. Then he told me what he had in mind. The idea seemed a little crazy at first. Neither of us ever dreamed that what happened next was even possible.

10

Stepping onto the Roller Coaster

KAELIN:

Life with Kaelin had hit a ceiling. You can do two things with a ceiling: either you can let it stop you and live with where you are, or you can bust through it and push to see if the sky is the limit. I chose the latter. However, I needed more than resolve. I had to have a plan. That sent me back into research mode. I studied couples who vlogged together and found some had millions of views. Those with the most didn't just vlog their lives. They also produced some viral content by pulling pranks on each other. That gave me an idea.

I dug a little deeper into the channels of successful couples. At the time, nearly all the really successful YouTube couples were white. I didn't see that as a problem. Instead, I saw it as an opportunity for Kyrah and me. I did find a handful of couples of color who vlogged and pulled pranks, but their approach was completely different than what I wanted to do. The simplest way to put it is this: These couples did pranks that should have come with an R rating. Since we were Christ followers, I wanted to produce something parents wouldn't mind letting their kids watch: videos that entertained while also being uplifting and encouraging. However, I wanted to avoid making some corny, cringeworthy, "Christian" knockoff of other videos. We had to have an edge, the kind where people have to share our videos with their friends, but I didn't want the edge to come with screaming profanity or just being nasty toward each other. I watched some couples do horrible things to each other, all in the name of racking up views, and I wondered how many relationships actually survived it.

Finally, after weeks of research, I came up with an idea for a prank to share with Kyrah. I thought it had potential. I hoped she could see it too.

KYRAH:

"You want me to do what?" was my first reaction when Kaelin told me his prank video idea.

"Throw my new iPhone into my pool," he replied.

"I'm not going to ruin your new phone," I said.

"You won't ruin it. It'll be sealed up inside the box where the water can't get to it," Kaelin said.

"But if it's in the box, what's the point? No one gets a new phone and leaves it in the box. You have it out before you leave the store. No one will believe this is real," I said.

"Don't worry. If you and I buy into it, people will believe us. Trust me."

I still wasn't completely convinced when I showed up at Kaelin's house one Saturday afternoon to do the video. "So, I'm going to be downstairs taking a nap," he explained, "and you'll sneak in and grab the bag with my phone in it, wake me up, and then head toward the pool. I'll wake up and chase you, but I won't catch you before you throw the phone in. Then I'll jump in the pool in my clothes to save it."

"So I just walk in, grab it, wake you up, run outside, and throw it in the pool?" I said.

"No, you'll talk about what you are going to do before you do it. You have to set the whole thing up first," he said.

"What do I say?" I said. "I'm not really the kind of person to throw my boyfriend's phone in the pool."

"Okay, let's just plan it out," Kaelin said. The two of us sat down and basically wrote a script for me. I then followed Kaelin out to the pool, where we set up cameras to catch everything from different angles. I had to hold the main camera, which is something I hated doing, but I didn't have a choice since I was the one pulling the prank. "How believable will it be if I hold the camera while being pranked?" Kaelin explained.

"It still feels, I don't know, dishonest. How is this a prank if we write everything out ahead of time?" I said.

"None of the pranks on YouTube are real," Kaelin said. "If they were, none of the couples doing them would still be together. They'd probably be in court or something."

That made me feel a little better. Basically, this video was all about entertainment, which made us entertainers like actors and actresses. I could do that, I hoped.

Once we had all the details worked out, we started shooting the video. I have to say, I felt really self-conscious making it. It didn't help that some of Kaelin's family was home while we made the video. At one point, we had to reshoot an entire scene when his dad walked into the kitchen talking really loud on his phone. Another time we had to stop the cameras when his brother walked out to the pool, looked around for a moment, then said, "Are y'all shooting a video out here?" Kaelin and I both looked at each other and said, "Yes!"

After a full day of shooting, Kaelin spent the night editing the video. We turned around and shot a couple more pranks, including one where Kaelin "tricked" me into eating dirt and another where I dumped an entire bag of flour over his head. The last one taught us a valuable lesson: flour doesn't wash away very easily. There's probably still flour embedded in the concrete of my parents' old house where we filmed it. Kaelin also pulled a real prank where he put a frog in a pizza box and brought it to me in the CSUB library, where I was studying. I thought something might be up when he walked in with his camera in hand, but I never expected him to put the one thing I am afraid of more than anything else in a box and hand it to me to open. That was the first—and the last—real prank he ever pulled on me. If he'd put another frog in a box, he would have had to find a new girlfriend to pull pranks on.

KAELIN:

I posted "Crazy Girlfriend Throws iPhone 7 in the Pool!!!," "Making Girlfriend Eat Dirt Prank," and "Song Lyric Prank on Girlfriend Gone Wrong" within a couple of days of each other in mid-September 2016. Each got a couple thousand views, which was basically what we averaged with our vlogs. I'd be lying if I said I wasn't disappointed. Other "crazy person throws something expensive into a swimming pool" videos piled up hundreds of thousands and millions of views. We got two thousand our first day. I still thought prank videos could help us crack the code to going viral. We made a few more and posted them the next week. All the while, I kept checking numbers.

Something odd started to happen. I checked our numbers multiple times a day. The iPhone prank's numbers kept going up. By the third day, it had five thousand views, which was very uncharacteristic for our channel. Usually we'd have a couple of thousand views the first day, and the video would sort of die after that. By the time I released our second batch of prank videos, the crazy girlfriend iPhone video had over fifteen thousand views. That video didn't die...The views kept slowly trickling in. I started to get excited.

The next week, Kyrah and I were in the library studying. However, I found it hard to concentrate on this particular day because every time I refreshed our YouTube channel page, our views and subscribers would jump by hundreds. I kept trying to focus on studying for midterms, but I just couldn't stay off my laptop. Our subscribers had jumped by more than two thousand since I had last looked earlier that day. I was blown away. I spun my laptop around and pointed at the number. "Kyrah," I tried to whisper. We were in the library, but I was too excited to keep my voice down completely. "We just gained two thousand subscribers in the last two hours." It had taken me over a year to get to two thousand alone, and we just did it in a matter of hours.

For some reason she didn't seem that excited.

I clicked around on the page and looked up our views. Total views on all our videos had jumped by hundreds of thousands. "Kyrah," I said, pointing to the screen, "we just made more while sitting here studying than you make in a month at your job!"

"How?" Kyrah asked.

"YouTube pays us for the ads they attach to the video. The more views, the more money we make. We've been here in the library for about two hours, and in that time, we've gained three hundred thousand views. That means we've made somewhere between one and two thousand dollars."

"*We* made that much money? It's your channel, not mine," she said.

"We did this together," I told her. "It's *our* money. I don't plan on touching a dime of it until after we get married."

Her expression changed when I said that. She looked relieved. She still didn't get as excited as I did about the numbers. When our views hit the millions and our subscribers came in so fast that we became, at that time, one of the fastest-growing channels ever on YouTube, she started to share my excitement.

Me, I wanted to pour gasoline on this fire. We'd already gone from posting once a week to daily. I decided to go up from there. However, it wasn't fair of me to ask Kyrah to make that kind of commitment when she already had a part-time job to go along with school. So, I made her an offer I believed was going to be the best investment ever. I asked her to quit her job and start doing YouTube full-time with me. At first, she was hesitant. I got it. Her dad wasn't paying for everything like he had her first year, which meant she had to work to pay for her gas and books and anything else she needed while going to school.

"What if I pay you what you'd make working retail?" I asked her. I then handed her an envelope with $3,000 in cash from money I'd saved while working at the credit union. She looked at me with a shocked expression. "I'm all in on this and I want you to be too. We may also want to consider putting school on hold for a while. This is a once-in-a-lifetime opportunity," I said. "This could literally change our lives."

I could never have imagined how true that last statement would turn out to be.

KYRAH:

The numbers on our channel really didn't mean much to me until one day a girl stopped me in the hall on the way to one of my classes. "Wait. Are you Kyrah?" she asked with a huge smile on her face.

"Um, yeah," I answered, trying to figure out where I might know her from. She could have been in one of my classes, but if so, we'd never met.

"Oh. My. Gosh. I watch you on YouTube!" she said like she could hardly believe I was me.

"That's amazing! Thank you!" I replied, kind of embarrassed by the attention. I didn't really know how to respond.

"Can I get a picture with you?" she asked, excited.

"Of course," I said.

She jumped to my side and took a quick selfie, then sort of squealed with excitement as she took off for her class, thanking me the whole way.

That was so weird, I thought to myself as I went on to my class. I walked the same hallways every day, and had for the past year and a half, but no one had ever stopped me before. *Why are they stopping me now?* I felt very uncomfortable with the attention. Kaelin and I now had a string of viral videos, but that didn't make me a celebrity. I was the same girl I had been the first day of class. *Why did anyone want a selfie with me?* It made no sense.

A couple of weeks later, my life as a student took an even stranger turn. Since our first video went viral, Kaelin and I had talked about possibly putting school on hold for a while and pouring all of our energy into our channel to see how far we could take it. I was hesitant. After all, I liked my college experience, and as the first person in my family to go to college, I wanted to finish. "I'm not saying we'll quit school forever," Kaelin said. "Who knows how long this wave we're riding will last? When it ends, we'll go back and finish what we started. But I think we owe it to ourselves to see how big we can make it while we can. How many people get an opportunity like this?"

By this point we had made more money than I had ever imagined possible, and we hadn't spent any of it. If we kept doing that, or at least only took out enough to live on, we could save enough that when we started going back to school, neither of us would have to work another job. That sounded good to me. "If we do this," I said to Kaelin, "I have to keep the door open to coming back here. I'm not going to quit in the middle of this semester and end up having to take all these classes over again, or, even worse, have them mess up my GPA to the point where I can't come back."

"I agree," Kaelin said. "We finish this semester and then start working YouTube full-time."

On my last day as a student at CSUB, I had one last final to take in my philosophy class. I wanted to do well and end school on a high note. At the time, Kaelin and I didn't know how long our string of successful videos might last. When we talked about leaving school, we both agreed we needed to end well to keep the door open if we ever wanted to go back. As far as we knew, we might need to come back after Christmas break for the start of the spring semester. When it comes to social media and the internet, nothing is ever certain.

I'd studied hard for this test. Part of me didn't want it to be the last test I ever took. Since I was the first person in my family to go to college, I hated not graduating on time. However, you go to college to open up options for your future and hopefully step into a good career. While YouTube personalities don't have the longest shelf life in the world, we now made enough to think of it as a career path, at least for a while. We now had nearly a million subscribers, even though we were only doing this part-time. Who knew what might happen if we put all of our time and energy into it?

Kaelin and I were also talking seriously about marriage. Actually, the conversation had started a year earlier when we'd nearly eloped, and it hadn't stopped since then. He hadn't yet proposed, but I knew it was only a matter of time. With what we were now earning from YouTube, money wasn't going to be a problem going forward, not for a while, at least.

With all of this racing through my head, I found it hard to concentrate on philosophy as I walked into class for my final. I found a seat, pulled a pencil out of my backpack, and tried to calm my mind before the professor walked in and handed us the test. The class was small, with maybe twenty students in the room. All of us had been here together for months, which made me do a double take when I noticed several girls had taken their phones out and were pointing them at me. I turned to see what they might be taking pictures of, but there was nothing there. Only me. *Nah, they can't be taking pictures of me,* I thought.

But the looks on their faces and their little "Oh my gosh, I can't believe it's her" giggles told me they were. I was literally five seats from them, close enough that any one of them could have said something like, "We watch you on YouTube," but they didn't. Instead, they kept taking photos and recording until the professor came in and told everyone to put their phones away. I acted like I didn't notice what they were doing, but I did. A few months earlier, my classmates had no idea who I was. Now they were starstruck. The whole thing was unreal.

As soon as the test was over, I grabbed my stuff, walked out of the classroom, and never looked back. The decision to step away from school for a while never looked better. *If these girls act like this because some of our videos went viral, what will happen if the channel really takes off?*

11

Ready to Take the Next Step

KYRAH:

One afternoon, Kaelin and I were hanging out in his "office," which was just a spare room in his parents' house, like we did every day. I don't remember if we were planning our next video or if he was editing one we'd just finished or both. We never stopped doing either since in those days we'd post one or two videos a day.

I don't remember exactly what we were talking about, but Kaelin said something like, "When we get married..."

I cut him off and joked, "Well, if you're going to marry me, you better move out of your parents' house first."

Kaelin laughed and said, "Don't test me. I'll go online right now and start looking for an apartment."

"You wouldn't know where to start," I said with a smile.

"You don't think so?" Kaelin said. "I'll go there right now."

"Where?" I asked.

"The complex right down the street where my brother lives," he said.

I laughed. "There's no way they have anything available. That place is too nice to have any vacancies."

"We'll see," he said as he typed away on his laptop. After a few minutes, he pushed back in his chair and looked at me wide-eyed, with a huge smile on his face. "Kyrah...I think I found the perfect apartment."

I didn't believe him until I saw it myself. His brother's apartment complex had a two-bedroom, two-bath unit available. "Just because there's a unit available doesn't mean we'll be able to get it," I said with a laugh.

"Only one way to find out," Kaelin said. He tapped on a few keys, then said, "Here's the application..." He then started typing fast.

"What are you doing?" I asked.

"Filling it out," he said without looking up. "And now it's sent," he said a few minutes later.

Maybe five minutes later his email alert dinged. "Whoa...," Kaelin said.

"What?"

"We got approved."

My heart jumped. What had started out as a game had suddenly become very real. I thought for a moment and said, "Well, I'll have to see it first. I'm not going to live just anywhere."

"But we've been in my brother's apartment a million times," Kaelin said. The two of us hung out there a lot. His brother had much better Wi-Fi than Kaelin's parents. We uploaded most of our videos there.

"That's not the same." I laughed.

"Well let's go see it," Kaelin said.

On the drive over to the apartment complex, neither of us thought any of this was real. Kaelin and I were only nineteen. Neither of us had any kind of long-term credit established, and we'd only been making money with our channel for about three months. There's no way any apartment manager would rent a place to us, although both of us were ready to get out on our own. There was a lot of tension in my house between my parents. Lately there had been more between my mom and me as well. The more time I spent away from her, the more I saw how she tried to manipulate me through guilt or by just wearing me down to do what she wanted. I did my best to spend as little time at home as possible. I knew Kaelin was also itching to move out of his parents' house. His dad had recently told him that since he was making good money on YouTube, he needed him to help with bills. When Kaelin told me about it, he said that if he had to pay to live somewhere, he'd rather pay to live in his own place. However, he'd never actually looked into finding a place until now. But it wasn't his place we were about to look at—it was ours. At least, eventually it was going to be ours. If we got an apartment, one of us would need to live there until we actually got married, whenever that might be. Soon, I hoped.

Honestly, I didn't think that was something either of us had to worry about because I thought there was no way we could get an apartment. I was certain we couldn't get one when we met with the apartment manager. She looked over our paperwork with a skeptical look on her face. That is, until Kaelin mentioned his brother lived there. "Oh, and who is he?" the manager asked, still very skeptical.

"He's the one who drives the red Lamborghini parked outside," Kaelin said.

The manager's whole tone changed. "So, you two do the same thing he does?" she asked.

"Yes, we do," Kaelin said.

She gave us an apartment that day, along with a January 25 move-in date. But that date was not for both of us. We decided Kaelin would take the apartment first, and I'd move in after we got married. That day could not get here fast enough for me, but there was just one problem: Kaelin still hadn't proposed. I wondered what he was waiting on. I felt like I was reliving the unnecessary boyfriend/girlfriend label drama from our junior year of high school. Back then, my friends had all said Kaelin had commitment issues. I'd never thought that was true, but then again, he kept talking about being married someday without actually asking me to, you know, *marry him!* I started to wonder if my friends had been right.

KAELIN:

I hadn't bought a ring when we signed the lease for the apartment, but I was in the middle of doing some serious shopping for one. I still thought I might be able to find the perfect ring for very little money since I was running low on the savings from my credit union days earlier that year. I still had not touched the money we were making on YouTube, and after investing in this new business, things were getting tight. Some dreams die slow and painful deaths, and my dream of a really cheap engagement ring died a little more every time I went shopping. By the time I happened to take Kyrah into a jewelry store—not for any reason, just because, uh, well, we were in the neighborhood—my hope of finding one within my budget was hanging by a thread. The salesperson who just happened to wait on us that day had helped me narrow my choices down to three possibilities a couple of days earlier. One of the three rings came really close to my budget, but when I saw it on Kyrah's finger, I threw my budget out the window. The next day I went back to the store by myself and bought the ring Kyrah loved the most, which also happened to be the one ring she'd never in a million years expect me to buy because of the price.

Now I needed to find the perfect place and time to pop the question.

Finding the right approach was a little tricky because we'd already talked about marriage so often, going back to our intentions talk before we ever went out on our first date. Yet, no matter how much Kyrah and I had talked about getting married in the past, moving from talk to actually asking her to marry me was a huge step. We'd both remember the moment for the rest of our lives. I wanted to make it special but not over the top. My friend Brandon volunteered his mom's cabin in Frazier Park in the mountains between Bakersfield and Los Angeles. The tall trees and mountain scenery were exactly what I was looking for. Brandon and I had spent a few days there a year earlier to ring in the New Year, and it was just beautiful. It was also incredibly quiet at that elevation. There's nothing up there but you, your thoughts, and nature. It was the perfect place to propose so that we could focus on each other and reflect on our relationship. Brandon also agreed to drive us up, along with his girlfriend, Jessica, to make it look to Kyrah like nothing more than a fun New Year's Eve day trip to the mountains. Kyrah and I could not go alone because my old car couldn't make it up the mountain and I needed Brandon there to video everything for me.

I didn't breathe a word to Kyrah until the day before. Then I casually said something like, "Hey, what do you think about going up to Brandon's mom's cabin with him and Jessica for New Year's Eve? We can all hang out, play board games, and watch movies. It should be fun."

Kyrah looked at me like she knew something was up. I hate the cold. Frazier Park was pretty high up in the mountains. In the summer you went to a place like that to get away from the heat, but you don't go in the winter. Besides, we'd been ring shopping. She knew I had to propose sometime soon, especially since we were scheduled to take possession of the apartment in a little over three weeks. "Okay. I'll ask my parents," she said.

"All right," I said. "We'll go up in the morning and get home before New Year's tomorrow night." I didn't want to leave too early because I had an errand to run first.

KYRAH:

When Kaelin brought up going to the cabin with Brandon and Jess, I was pretty certain he planned to propose up there. However, I didn't think he'd propose without a ring, and I knew he hadn't had a chance to go buy one.

The two of us were together every waking moment of every day. The more I thought about going up to the cabin, the more annoyed and stressed out I started to become. What was even the point of going up there without a ring?! I was starting to feel like he was just leading me on, especially after taking me ring shopping a few weeks earlier.

I hardly slept that night. I got up around six and texted Kaelin, telling him I was ready to leave whenever he was. The plan was to leave early in the morning, but it took him forever to text me back and even longer for him to give me the okay that I could go pick him up. I knew we'd been out late the night before, so maybe he was just sleeping in. I started to worry that the entire plan had fallen through since no one kept me updated.

KAELIN:

I got up early and arrived at the jewelry store as soon as it opened. I'd already bought the ring the day after Kyrah and I had gone, but they had to size it before I could pick it up. When I opened the box to take another look before I left the store, the reality of what was about to happen hit me. I had a loose idea of what I was going to do. I'd take Kyrah outside, get down on one knee, pop the question, then bring out the ring. However, I had no idea what I was going to say. I knew I needed to say something from the heart, but my mind just went kind of blank as I tried to plan it out.

We decided to meet Brandon and Jessica at a gas station in Frazier Park so we could hop in Brandon's car before going up the mountain, since it was the only car able to drive on the slick roads. Until Brandon texted me telling me he was on his way, I didn't know for certain if we'd get to use the cabin. My mind kept tripping, trying to come up with a plan B of where to do this, just in case. I was very relieved when he told me that we had the cabin.

KYRAH:

I knew something was up the moment I climbed into the back seat of Brandon's car next to Kaelin. Jessica looked back at me with this huge smile on her face. "Hey, Jess," I said.

"Hey, Kyrah," she said, barely able to speak she was smiling so hard.

If the way everyone acted when I got in the car didn't give it away, the way Kaelin held my hand certainly did. He grabbed it with both hands and could not stop smiling at me. I kept thinking, *This is really happening*, but I didn't say anything to let on that I was in on the surprise.

KAELIN:

Sitting in the back seat of Brandon's car, holding on to Kyrah's hand, I started to think back on how we got to this point. "I date to marry," I'd declared before I ever asked Kyrah out on a date. Now here we were, three years later, with me about to ask her to be my wife. I was excited and nervous, but more than anything, I felt an overwhelming sense of gratitude to God for bringing Kyrah and me together. Sitting in the car on the drive up to Brandon's mom's cabin, the words of Ephesians 5:25 ran through my mind: "Husbands, love your wives, as Christ loved the church and gave himself up for her." That verse tells me that my love for Kyrah must be a crucifixion kind of love, the love that moved Jesus to stretch out his arms on the cross. In between gazing into Kyrah's eyes, thinking about how I was the luckiest guy on earth right then, I asked God to lead me as I committed to loving her for the rest of my life.

I hadn't planned anything special for the proposal. I wanted intimacy with no distractions. I didn't have rose petals to spread out on the ground or candles to spell out "Will you marry me?" I had not invited our families up to the cabin to share in the moment, nor had I hired a guy with a guitar to play "our" song. I had not planned anything but a simple proposal with no special effects. God took care of those. As we arrived at the cabin, it started to snow. I looked up at the snow gently falling from the sky, and I knew that I could never have planned anything more magical than this moment God had prepared for us.

I didn't grab Kyrah and pop the question as soon as we arrived. All four of us went into the cabin, and I did my best to act like we were just going to hang out. But I couldn't keep it up. After a couple of minutes, I said, "We should probably go get some firewood, don't you think, Brandon?"

"Oh yeah," he said, and the two of us went outside to set up the shot so that Brandon could capture the moment for us to cherish forever.

KYRAH:

Jessica and I sat in the cabin, neither one of us talking, just sort of staring at each other. I was too excited to talk. Even though Kaelin and I had talked seriously about getting married for over a year, I was still in shock that he was about to ask me to be his wife. I started to ask Jessica if she knew for sure what Kaelin had planned, but I didn't. If he was going to propose, I didn't want to spoil the surprise. And if he wasn't, I didn't want to know that yet. So, instead of talking, we sat there, waiting.

Finally, Kaelin stuck his head in the door and said, "Kyrah, can you give me a hand with something?"

I looked over at Jessica with an excited smile and said, "Sure."

I grabbed Kaelin's hand and followed him over toward an open area a little ways from the cabin. By now, the snow had started falling harder. Even though I didn't have a heavy coat on, I was too excited to be cold. We walked a short way, and then he stopped and turned toward me. "Kyrah," he said before dropping down to one knee.

When he went to one knee, I was speechless. It's one thing to suspect your boyfriend is going to propose, and another to see him drop to one knee before your eyes. I kept thinking, *WHAT ARE WE DOING?!* My entire future flashed before my eyes while Kaelin told me how much he loved me and wanted to spend the rest of his days loving me. I thought about how much he cared for me and championed me every day of our relationship. I knew I would be the happiest bride marrying the man of my dreams.

The moment the words "Will you marry me?" came out of his mouth, I said, "Yes!" Everything felt so unreal, like I needed someone to pinch me. I couldn't even find it in me to cry. I was so unbelievably happy.

Then Kaelin took out the ring box and opened it up. "Is that the ring?!" I said.

"Yes, this was your top choice." Kaelin laughed. He then slipped the ring onto my finger.

Kaelin stood up and I threw my arms around him. Both of us were so happy. We didn't care that the snow was pouring down on us now. We wanted to soak in every moment.

I looked around. We were both shivering, but up until then I didn't notice how cold I was. We kissed again and then I grabbed his hand and we ran back to the cabin.

KAELIN:

The plan was for us to drive back down to Bakersfield right after I proposed. However, the light, perfect snow that had given us some incredible pictures now started pouring down. It doesn't snow in Bakersfield. Ever. I had never seen snow in my life, much less driven in it. Brandon hadn't prepared to drive in snow. Several inches had piled up, and it wasn't slowing down. "What do you think?" I asked him.

"I don't know. Let's wait a while and see if it slows down. The roads up here are sketchy enough without snow," Brandon said.

We waited an hour. Several inches of snow had now become a couple of feet. Brandon was pretty sure they plowed the roads up here, but we hadn't heard any plows and we sure didn't want to drive in the snow after dark. "I think we're probably going to be stuck up here until it stops," Brandon said.

I knew Brandon was right, but I hated the optics of all of us spending the night in a cabin while dating and newly engaged. For two people who'd talked a lot about purity in our videos, that didn't look good. "Where are we going to sleep?" I asked.

"There's only one bedroom," Brandon said. "The girls can take the room and we can crash on the couch in the living room."

"Sounds good to me," I said.

The four of us stayed up talking, eating, and playing board games. We celebrated the New Year by watching the ball drop on television. None of us were ready to go to bed, so we put on a movie as the four of us all crowded on the couch. A few minutes into the movie, Brandon and Jessica passed out asleep on the couch. Kyrah and I cozied closer together and watched the movie. Both of us were still over the moon from the proposal. Neither of us wanted the night to end.

When the movie ended, Kyrah and I moved off the couch and onto a blanket on the floor. We kissed and we held each other, and one thing led to another until it almost led us too far. Both of us had let our guard down, which put us both in a very vulnerable position. We stopped ourselves, but barely.

Afterward, I lay there in the dark thinking about how we'd gone from such an incredible high, a moment where we'd felt God's smile upon us, to nearly compromising ourselves and our testimonies. We'd talked so much about waiting until we were married to have sex, and here we had nearly blown that commitment with the finish line in sight. It wasn't the last night we struggled with self-control. After I moved into the apartment, we had a few other moments of being alone that almost led us further than we wanted to go.

Looking back at this night, and some that followed, I realize our purity was more of an ideal we told ourselves than a reality in our lives. No, we did not have sex until after we were married, but we came so close before that we cannot look down on anyone who stumbles in this area. Yes, God has reserved sex for marriage, but He also offers grace and forgiveness for all who repent and turn to Him. Some people scare others into believing that they're eternally blemished by the mistakes they make. Most commonly we see this by those who make it seem as if those who haven't had sex before marriage are pure, but the rest are forever impure. I don't think that's how it really works. We don't even make ourselves pure in the first place! All of us have sinned against God and fallen short of His perfect standard. This reality is important because all sin has a cost, and that price is death. Although we deserve death for all of our sins, God has extended grace and mercy to cover the cost for us. God sent His Son, Jesus, to atone for the sins of humanity. That's a free gift that's available to all who repent, believe, and follow Him. Now, true purity is not based off any sexual technicalities of what we do or don't do. True purity is sealed for eternity through Jesus and what He has done. God is perfect and acts as a substitute to atone for our sinfulness. It's Jesus's sacrificial love that has redeemed us and made us pure in Him and in His eyes. That's far more pure than any technicality could ever make you! Since we love Him, we should strive to follow His perfect design for our relationships and especially our lives. Yet, when we fall short, we can be assured that there is no condemnation for those in Christ. Following Jesus is not about taking advantage of His grace and doing what we want. If we truly love Him, we'll strive to keep His commandments, knowing that even when we fail, He will give us the room to grow and make mistakes while He shapes us into who He is calling us to be.

12

What Are We Waiting On?

KYRAH:

"Are we really going to do this?" I asked, nervous. Kaelin and I had stayed up most of the previous night talking about getting married right away, not several months down the road. He had moved into the apartment two weeks earlier, which was three weeks after we got engaged.

Kaelin may have lived there, but except for overnight, I might as well have moved in too. At this point, I wasn't getting along with my parents at all, especially my mom. We were having that battle I think a lot of teenagers go through when we realize we're becoming adults and are ready to begin making decisions for ourselves. After I got engaged, I felt like my mom projected even more of her frustration with my dad onto Kaelin. He couldn't do much right in her eyes. It didn't help when I talked Kaelin into getting a couple of kittens. Long story short: Kaelin didn't want pets, but I did, so he agreed to do a trial run. It did not go well, and the two of us decided, together, after long talks and many tears, that we would rehome the kittens. It was important to me to uphold my end of the deal, and I knew it would really set the precedent in our marriage concerning compromises and keeping our word. We rehomed them, and that was the last straw for my mom. "He has no right to do that!" she yelled at me.

"We agreed to rehome them," I explained.

"He's just controlling you. You didn't agree to anything. He knows how to make you do whatever he wants," she blew up.

I blew up back at her, and by the time Kaelin and I returned to the apartment later that night, I told Kaelin I wanted to get married the next day. "We are going to get married anyway, so why not do it now?" I said. "What are we waiting on? I don't care about having a big wedding. I just want to be married."

Later that night, we went back to my parents' house to grab my boxes. On both the drive over and the drive back, we discussed the idea of getting married the next day. The plan made sense to us then. I wondered if maybe he'd have a change of heart after sleeping on it.

But the next morning, our resolve hadn't changed.

"I'm still ready if you are," Kaelin said. He looked at me with a smile on his face and added, "I can't wait to marry you."

"I can't wait either! I guess we're getting married today! We have a lot to do...," I said.

KAELIN:

I called my dad first thing, not for his permission but for his guidance. Growing up as a pastor's kid, I remembered many times when people had called my dad at some odd hour and asked him to perform a hurry-up wedding. That's why I was pretty sure we could pull this wedding off in one day. I'd seen it happen.

"Hey, Dad," I said when he answered his phone.

"What's wrong?" my mom asked. Apparently, my mom and dad were in his car and he had me on speaker.

"Why do you ask what's wrong?" I said.

"Because you haven't called us since you moved out of our house two weeks ago," my mom said.

"Sorry about that," I replied. "I've been really busy trying to get everything set up in the apartment. Anyway, Dad, I wanted to talk to you about me and Kyrah. We want to get married today. What do we need to do?"

"Why so fast?" my dad shot back. "Y'all been playin' house?" My parents don't sugarcoat anything.

"No, nothing like that," I said. "I mean, Kyrah has been over here so late a couple of times that she fell asleep and didn't wake up until the next morning."

"So, y'all shackin' up," my mom said.

"No, we're not, and we don't plan to. That's why we want to go ahead and get married now," I said.

"Now? Like today?" my dad asked, but not in a surprised tone. I'd had a bunch of conversations with him about me marrying Kyrah over the past two years. He had a pretty good idea the two of us wouldn't wait long after I finally proposed.

"Yeah, today," I said. Kyrah not wanting to go home wasn't the only reason we wanted to get married right away. With so much time alone together, I didn't know how much longer we could control ourselves with each other. That's one of the reasons why we wanted to get married now, before hormones and opportunity got the better of us.

"Okay, we can do that down at the church later," my dad said. "But first you're gonna need to go to the courthouse and get a license. Can't marry you legally without a license," he added.

"We will go this morning," I said. "Will seven tonight work for the wedding? We only want a few people there but they're gonna need to get off work."

"Seven is fine."

"And can you let the rest of the family know?" I asked.

"Sure," my dad said. "We'll see y'all tonight at seven."

KYRAH:

As soon as Kaelin hung up with his parents, we headed straight for the courthouse. The problem was neither of us had ever been there before. Even with GPS, we still felt lost most of the drive over. Finding the courthouse wasn't the only thing I was worried about. I didn't know what documents we might need to get a marriage license. Did I need to stop by my parents' house to get my birth certificate? What about my social security card? I looked at the clock. I wished we hadn't stayed up most of the night talking about doing this and then slept so late in the morning. I sighed, thinking we would run out of time.

KAELIN:

Once we found the courthouse, I had no idea where we were supposed to go to get a marriage license. Kyrah and I wandered around the lobby like a couple of lost kids at an amusement park. I spotted a police officer and went over to him to ask for directions. "Excuse me. Can you tell me where to go to get married?" I asked like I was nine years old, not nineteen.

I fully expected the officer to give us the once-over and say something like, *What are you two doing here? You're too young to get married.* But he didn't. Instead, he smiled and said, "You need to go to the county clerk's office and they'll take care of you. It's right down that hall."

"Thank you, sir," I said, still feeling like a little kid.

I didn't feel much more confident when we walked into the Kern county clerk's office. "We want to get married," I told the woman behind the counter.

Again, I fully expected her to tell us that we were too young. To my surprise, she pointed to a computer monitor on the other side of the room. "You can fill out the application over there. Once you finish, you will hit 'submit'; then have a seat and I'll call you up when everything is ready."

"That's it?" I said.

"That and a twenty-five-dollar filing fee," she said.

Kyrah and I raced to fill out the license application. When we got to the bottom of the form and hit submit, I thought this was it, like we were saying, "I do." But then another page popped up, so I was like, "Ahhhh, I guess we're not married yet." A few minutes later, the clerk handed us the official certificate, and once again, I thought we were now married in the eyes of the state of California.

KYRAH:

After the clerk gave us the marriage license and we got back in our car, Kaelin called his dad and said, "Hey, Dad, we're married." I couldn't hear what his dad said, but I could tell by the look on Kaelin's face that his father had made it clear that we were not. "Okay, we're still on for seven tonight then, right. Okay, thanks, Dad. And did you let the rest of the family know... Thanks. We'll see you in a little bit."

When he hung up the phone, I said, "So we're not actually married yet?"

"Nope. That's the license that lets us get married. So now we need to get me a ring," he said.

"Can we eat lunch first? I'm so hungry," I said. By now it was close to two o'clock. "Also, I was thinking we should invite our friends, don't you think?"

"Oh, yeah…," Kaelin said. "But we're tight on time."

"Maybe we could ask one each. I really want Daja there."

"I'll ask Brandon. He was there for the engagement. Might as well have him here for the wedding too," Kaelin said with a laugh.

We texted them both during lunch. I was so happy when Daja said she could come. I also texted my parents, telling them what was happening and inviting them to come to the wedding. I didn't call. After the way the previous night had gone, I really didn't want to talk to my mom and have her try to talk me out of marrying Kaelin, although I hoped they'd come to the ceremony. Despite the argument the night before, I loved my parents and I wanted them there for the biggest day of my life.

After lunch, we headed straight to the jeweler where Kaelin had bought my ring. When we walked in, the salesclerk immediately recognized him. "You're back. Nice to see you. What can I help you with now?"

"We need to pick out my wedding band," she said.

"Okay, wonderful," the clerk said. "And when is the wedding?"

"In about four hours," I said.

The clerk did a double take. "Today? You're getting married today?" she said.

"Yes," I said.

"Okay, then let me show you two some options."

KAELIN:

Kyrah and I followed the clerk to the men's section. I assumed picking out a ring might take five, maybe ten minutes, tops. After all, how long can it take to pick out a men's wedding band? The answer, I learned, was a lot longer than five or ten minutes. I had no idea there were so many different styles and materials to choose from. Because I needed the ring that day, our choices were also limited to what they had in stock.

Finally, we settled on a simple tungsten band. But I couldn't take the ring with me. "We will need to size it for you," the clerk told me. When she measured my finger, she came up with a size eight, but there was a catch. "You're young so you may want the bigger size so that you can grow into it," the clerk said. Once again, I felt like I was a kid buying school clothes with my mom. She'd always bought my pants a little too big so that I wouldn't outgrow them before the end of the school year. Now the jeweler recommended the same thing for my wedding band.

"Okay, sure, that's fine," I said. "We just need it in time for our wedding at seven tonight." The clerk assured me that was not a problem. I had my doubts. The sun was already starting to go down. Sure, it was February and days are pretty short, but still, this day was flying by.

KYRAH:

My choice of what to wear for my wedding was limited to what I could dig out of one of the boxes we'd brought over the night before. That's the beauty of planning a wedding in eight hours. You don't have time to worry about any of the details.

I started getting ready while Kaelin went into the living room and lay down. I think he was trying to take a nap. I was too excited to sleep. We had the license. Kaelin already had my ring from when he bought the engagement ring. If the jewelry store did what they'd promised, we'd have Kaelin's ring soon. We had the church and the minister, who just so happened to be my future father-in-law. Barring a massive earthquake or some other catastrophe, we were about to get married!

KAELIN:

It was already nearly seven o'clock by the time we drove back to the jewelry store. The church was in the opposite direction, so this extra stop wasn't exactly on the way. "I hope your ring is ready," Kyrah said.

"If it's not, it's no big deal. We'll still be just as married," I said. Kyrah smiled. The reality of what was about to happen was finally starting to hit me.

My ring was ready…barely. When I put it on, it was still warm from where they'd resized and cleaned it. But it didn't fit. The ring hung down from my finger like I'd put on one of my dad's suits. "This is way too big," I told the salesclerk who'd sold us the ring.

"Better to be too big than too small. Don't worry. You'll grow into it," she said with a smile.

Whatever, I thought. We didn't have time to argue with her. My choices were either get married with a ring that was too big or get married with no ring at all. We thanked her for rushing the order and ran back to the car. We were going to be late for our own wedding. "Don't worry," I reassured Kyrah. "It's not like they can start without us."

KYRAH:

I could not believe my eyes when we walked through the doors of Kaelin's dad's church. Up on the big screen in the front, a video was playing, showing photographs of Kaelin and me together through the years. I nearly cried. "Who did this?!" I asked.

"Kelsie," Kaelin's mom said. Kelsie is his older sister. I hugged her and thanked her for doing something to make this day extra special. Before we arrived at the church, Kaelin and I expected the wedding ceremony to be nothing but the two of us exchanging "I dos." The video made the moment feel like an actual wedding.

My parents and siblings were already seated when we walked in. In spite of what had happened the night before, seeing them there made me so happy. I didn't know if their feelings about Kaelin had changed, but they both had smiles on their faces that at least made it look like they approved. It was as if the argument the night before had never happened.

When it came time for the ceremony to begin, Kaelin's dad, who was dressed in his black pastoral robes, led us up on the stage. He paused for a moment. "Daja...Brandon, I need the two of you to come up here with Kaelin and Kyrah." Both sort of shrugged and walked up front. Brandon was wearing shorts, and Daja hadn't dressed up either.

Kaelin leaned over toward his father and asked, "Why do you need them up here?"

"Can't have a wedding without a best man and maid of honor," he said.

Kaelin looked at me and smiled. "I agree," I said.

Once Daja and Brandon were in place, Kaelin's dad nodded toward Kelsie's fiancé, who was sitting at the piano. He began to play the wedding march. When the music ended, Kaelin's dad said, "Dearly beloved, we are here..." and then he went into his full wedding sermon.

And then we got to the part I'd waited so long to hear. "I now pronounce you husband and wife. You may kiss the bride," Kaelin's dad said. Hearing those words made my heart soar. The moment was...perfect.

KAELIN:

An old African tradition has the bride and groom jump over a broom as part of the wedding ceremony. After my dad pronounced us husband and wife, I took Kyrah by the hand, and we walked off the stage and down the steps to the center aisle of the church as my future brother-in-law played exit music on the piano. A broom was waiting for us on the floor. Kyrah and I looked at each other for a moment, then jumped over. As soon as we did, I swept Kyrah up into my arms and headed toward the door. Holding her in my arms, walking down the aisle of the church as husband and wife, was everything I'd ever dreamed it could be.

Afterward, both our families went out to a local restaurant for dinner. This was the first time everyone in our families had ever been together.

When the check came, I snatched it before my dad or father-in-law could reach it, and of course they both reached for it. "I've got this," I said. They argued with me over it, but I insisted. "No, I appreciate the gesture, but this is my wedding. I'll pay for the meal." Paying that check felt like a huge coming-of-age moment, like in the eyes of my father and father-in-law, I was now ready to take care of my family going forward. Then I looked at the bill. *Wow, this wedding isn't quite as cheap as I thought it was going to be*, I laughed to myself.

KYRAH:

Kaelin and I went back to what was now officially *our* apartment to begin our happily ever after. Since we still planned to have a full wedding, we didn't tell anyone beyond our closest friends and family that we were married. Online we were still engaged. Personally, I really didn't need a second wedding, but my mom kept telling me I'd always dreamed of a big wedding, and I got tired of arguing with her over it. I had to admit that I did want the thrill of the long dress and seeing Kaelin dressed up in his tuxedo. I also liked the idea of an outdoor location and a professional photographer and videographer to record every second of it for us. We didn't have that for our first wedding.

However, Kaelin and I had our dream wedding our way six weeks after our first. Instead of renting a venue, we found a field on the outskirts of Bakersfield and had the ceremony there. We didn't even find it in advance and rent it out. A week or two before the wedding, we scouted out a few general possible sites and came across the perfect location. We literally drove around until we found a field that felt dreamy, texted our location to our family and friends, and did the service there. We didn't set out chairs or bring in flowers or anything extra people customarily do for a wedding. Springtime in California means rolling hills covered with a sheet of fresh green grass and sprinkled with wildflowers, and that was enough decoration for me. As the sun set, its golden rays made our make-shift outdoor venue resemble a charming countryside. The ceremony and everything else was simple and beautiful and perfect. The next day, Kaelin and I flew to Hawaii for our dream honeymoon.

I could not have been happier. I felt like I had everything I'd ever wanted. I also believed no two people could have been more prepared to be married than Kaelin and me. Little did I know the real work of blending two lives together was only now about to begin.

13

What Honeymoon Phase?

KYRAH:

I went into marriage thinking I was going to be fully known and fully loved by my husband. Before we got married, Kaelin was so affectionate. "I love yous" flowed as we held hands and talked about the future late into the night. Although we worked together full-time, work never got in the way of the more important parts of our relationship. I remember being so in love, so excited about saying, "I do," and never having to say goodbye to Kaelin at the end of the day again.

Then we got back from our honeymoon and Kaelin said, "Okay, back to work. We need to figure out what we're doing with the channels."

What happened to the romantic guy I married? I wondered. Honestly, I was in shock. Everyone told me that the first year of marriage is this incredible honeymoon phase where you are so in love and life feels like a dream come true. I don't know what these people were talking about. We had almost completely stopped being affectionate, and romance was something in movies, not our apartment. Before we got married, we couldn't keep our hands off each other. Now we could—Kaelin could, at least. I craved his caress. I wanted to be held. I wanted my husband, but more often than not, my sexual advances toward Kaelin were met with him rolling over and going to sleep. He often initiated intimacy, but rarely accepted my initiation. I wondered if something was wrong with me, if he somehow now found me unattractive. Kaelin assured me that was not the case. "What, then?" I asked. "What's the problem?"

"I don't know that there's really a problem," he said, which, of course, only made the problem worse. Some nights I lay awake in the dark, wondering if I'd made a huge mistake getting married so quickly. Had we mistaken lust for love? Was I nothing more than a challenge to be conquered? Now that he'd gotten what he'd wanted, did he no longer need to shower me with affection? We still had sex, but only when Kaelin initiated it. Even then, the romance and passion that had almost carried us too far when we were dating now seemed to be missing. Physical intimacy is supposed to be about giving ourselves to each other, but I felt like Kaelin didn't care about what I needed. Once he had what he wanted, he disengaged from me.

We didn't really talk about the problems in the bedroom. It was too embarrassing for me to bring up. The time or two when I did bring up how frustrated I was, Kaelin seemed surprised. "How am I supposed to know what you want if you won't tell me?" he asked. He was fully sincere when he said this. More than once, he literally asked me, "What do you want? Help me understand." I never had an answer because I didn't know. I just knew the present circumstances weren't working for me.

It wasn't just the physical expressions of love that suddenly seemed to be missing. We didn't talk like we had before we were married. Even in the weeks before our quick wedding ceremony, we'd stayed up most of the night talking about our hopes and our dreams and our future. After we returned home from our honeymoon, we still talked late into the night, but instead of talking about us, we talked about the channel and what we were going to do with our videos. It was like the business never ended, like work never stopped. I started to feel like a commodity, as if our only reason for being together was to produce content for our YouTube channel.

KAELIN:

I knew life was about to change when Kyrah and I got married, and I wasn't sure how to handle it. The transition into married life didn't have me stressed. I thought we basically made that transition when we started working together. No, the big life change that kept me up at night had to do with our YouTube channel. Since the Saturday afternoon when we'd filmed our first prank at my parents' house, I'd known this kind of content had a potentially short shelf life. When we posted the first few pranks on our channel, we just hoped one of them might go viral. After they *all* started to take off, we faced the question of how to top what we'd already done. We had to keep coming up with new and more shocking videos to keep the audience coming back for more. Every video had to make the stakes higher and our reactions bigger. Coming up with new ideas exhausted me.

Kyrah and I also became more uncomfortable with our increasingly sensational prank videos. From the start, the pranks were all an act. I assumed our audience understood that, or that they would pick up on the fact that these were fake pretty quick. Kyrah and I pulled a prank on each other every other day, and we always had such a huge, surprised reaction that I thought everyone had to know we were acting. But people didn't. The comments they left made it clear that most of our audience believed the pranks were real and that Kyrah was the kind of girl who'd throw a brand-new laptop on the barbecue grill and set it on fire and that I was the kind of guy who'd put my girlfriend through any kind of emotional distress just for a laugh. We thought about adding a disclaimer to make it clear that the pranks were an act, but that only solved the problem of us misleading our audience with lies.

The bigger problem with which we wrestled was the perception people had of us as a result of what they watched on our channel. Kyrah hated the idea that people believed she really was a crazy girlfriend, and I did not enjoy having people think that I'm this horrible, overly controlling person. The people we played in our prank videos are pretty much the exact opposite of who we really are. I can't blame our audience, though. People believe what they see with their own eyes. We tried to solve this problem by showing who we really were in our non-prank videos, where we vlogged and talked more about our relationship, but those were never as popular as the pranks. We felt like prisoners of our own success.

The pranks also affected our relationship with each other. Recording the pranks became such a pressure-filled experience that Kyrah often broke down in tears, saying I was too hard on her for not getting things right. I felt a wedge coming between us because of it. On top of everything, the pranks did not build the community I'd always dreamed of building. Any community we did build was completely polarized between Team Kyrah and Team Kaelin, neither of which was an actual representation of who we were. Rather than the videos where we pulled pranks on each other, both of us much preferred our more substantive videos on our vlog channel where we actually got to be ourselves. However, I hesitated to switch our main channel completely to that kind of content because, as the old saying goes, if it ain't broke, don't fix it, and millions of views per day told me that the sensational formula worked.

What I suspected about the long-term feasibility of a channel built on viral videos was confirmed when, about a month before I proposed to Kyrah, I received an email from a man who is today our manager. He had watched our channel and thought we had great potential. However, in our first conversation he said something that really took me aback. "You guys are hot right now," he said, "but we need to figure out a way to turn this virality into a business that's sustainable."

My first reaction was, *I don't know who you are to call me, the guy who has discovered the secret sauce and gets tens of millions of views per month, and tell me that our success won't last.* I didn't actually say that to him, and I'm glad I didn't because he was right. What goes up always comes down. That's especially true in the world of YouTube, where the burnout rate for content creators is through the roof. However, sensational content had brought us to where we were now. What could we possibly replace it with and still retain our audience? We were all in. We were married. We wanted to have a family. I'd tried a different approach before, and I'd topped out with a few thousand subscribers. Kyrah and I couldn't live on that.

What I did not realize until we had further conversations with him was that there were brands that wanted to invest in us, but only if we moved away from childish entertainment and more toward content that invited people to come in and do life with us. Brand sponsorships meant we could earn more with fewer viewers than we ever made with millions. It also meant that we would have contracted work, which is more predictable than income based on our shot-in-the-dark pranks. Moving away from pranks did not mean we had to become all serious all the time, he explained to us. People come to YouTube to be entertained and to have fun. But they also come there to connect, and that's what we lacked—real connections.

After numerous conversations that lasted long into the night, Kyrah and I decided not only to hire this manager who dared question my business strategy, but also to heed his advice. The day after we got home from our honeymoon, we made a video called "The End of Kaelin and Kyrah," which announced our transition away from pranks and into content that reflected the real us. The announcement shocked our audience and quickly surpassed one million views.

I have to be honest. Although I appeared resolute in the video, I was second-guessing the whole decision. Even though both of us knew this was the right move, my mind kept bouncing between *I hope this works* and *What are we thinking?!* By making this video, we effectively told a large portion of our audience we were done with them. Over the past six months, we'd had amazing growth in both views and subscribers. How many of them might stick around for the new journey?

Half?

A third?

None?

If our audience evaporated, how would I pay our bills? Yes, it was our channel, but I felt that as the husband my first responsibility was to provide financially for my family. The bills were on me, and we had more than I had counted on. Before we got married, I'd created what I thought was a detailed budget. That budget didn't survive a day. As soon as we returned to Bakersfield from our honeymoon, extra monthly expenses popped up. My dad forwarded my car insurance bills. Kyrah's dad sent over her insurance, along with a student loan payment I hadn't been aware of. The bills kept coming while our income was up in the air. I'd thought we had enough in savings to carry us until this new approach with our channel started to pay off. Now I wasn't so sure.

To me, there was only one solution: work harder. Our honeymoon was an incredible vacation, but the moment the wheels of the plane touched down in Bakersfield, the vacation was over and it was time to get to work. And I mean work. Our whole business was potentially in jeopardy, so I planned to do everything humanly possible to make sure our new strategy succeeded. Every night, I lay in bed coming up with new ideas to try, and in the morning, I woke up early thinking about how to get the job done. The deeply felt need to provide for my family drove me. It was all I could think about. Everything else came second. Everything.

KYRAH:

I used to daydream about what it was going to be like to wake up next to Kaelin. I thought we'd snuggle for a while or make love or just lie there and talk until we absolutely had to drag ourselves out of bed. Reality didn't quite measure up. Most mornings, the first words I heard were "It's time to get up so we can work."

"You can get up. I am going back to sleep" became my standard answer. The more Kaelin bugged me to get to work, the more determined I became to lie there as long as possible. Yeah, I was just being stubborn, but I also knew I hit him where it mattered most: work. Some days I basically didn't get up. I was awake and I got dressed, but I lay around watching shows on my laptop or playing on my phone. The problem went deeper than work. Marriage was not what I'd expected.

I wasn't growing.

I wasn't thriving.

I'd been thrown into the deep end of the pool and now I was floating along, miserable.

I should have said something, but I didn't. I didn't know what I'd say. I had trouble figuring out exactly what I felt inside. Kaelin seemed to be disengaged emotionally, which made it easy for me to blame him for how I felt. But it wasn't just him. It was me as well. In the months leading up to our wedding, I could not wait to get out of my parents' house. They didn't get along with each other, and I didn't get along with my mom. We never saw eye to eye about anything anymore. And yet, now that I was a married woman who had, in the words of Genesis 2:24, left my father and mother and become one with my husband, all I wanted to do was go home and hang out with my mom and my sisters. So that's what I did. Most days when I did manage to drag myself out of bed, I headed straight to my mom. I never planned to stay away long. I always told Kaelin I'd be right back. At first, "right back" was a couple of hours. Then it turned into half a day. Then all day. A night came where I texted Kaelin and told him I was too tired to drive home and was going to sleep at my mom's. I never stayed away more than one night, but even on the nights I didn't sleep there I'd sometimes stay late into the night.

Don't get me wrong. I loved Kaelin and wanted to spend time with him. However, I found it much easier to hang out with my sisters, baking cookies and watching Netflix, than face the responsibilities of work and bills and cleaning and everything else that comes with adulthood. I also carried my frustrations with me to my parents' house, and I wasn't shy about letting them spill to my mom. Whenever I complained about Kaelin and how distant I felt from him, my mom always took my side, just as she had when I was a kid. Nothing was ever my fault. She never told me to get back to my new home and talk to my husband and work through our problems before they grew so large they consumed our relationship. Instead, I was told how awful he was and how mistreated I was and how no one should have to put up with what he was putting me through.

When I went back to our apartment, I never talked to Kaelin about how I felt. He constantly asked what was bothering me. Instead of giving him an honest answer, I told him everything was fine, and I buried my feelings down and floated along. But you can only bury feelings for so long before they come rushing out, and I hit that point several months into our marriage.

Late one afternoon, I came home from my parents' house and planted myself on the couch in front of the TV. I spent a lot of time watching television, especially the show *The Bachelor*. The fantasy world of *The Bachelor* certainly didn't help in my spiraling toxic thoughts about my husband. I watched these amazing dream dates these people went on and the huge romantic gestures the men made, and I wondered why my husband wasn't doing the same for me. "What's wrong?" Kaelin asked.

"Nothing," I said.

"You're acting different than you used to," he said.

"I don't think so," I replied. "I'm fine. I had a great day at my mom's. Everything is good."

"You don't seem fine. You look exhausted. What's really going on, Kyrah? What's bothering you?"

I started tearing up.

"Kyrah, what's going on?"

This wasn't the first time Kaelin had pressed me about what was bothering me. He did that a lot. I never responded well because timing and tone are everything! When he asked me what was wrong, it was always around the same time he complained about me being too lazy to get out of bed and get to work. His tone, rather than offering me a safe space to speak what was on my mind, always sounded accusatory. He wanted to fix me, but then he turned around and nitpicked my every move. That made me clam up even more, which fed into a cycle of me becoming upset with him because he couldn't read my mind and know what was bothering me without me saying a word.

"Nothing. I'm fine," I said. Everything certainly was not fine, and it was more than Kaelin turning into a workaholic. Of course, now I look back and know exactly what the problem was and how I'd communicate it, but at the time I couldn't really put my finger on the exact issue. I just knew that something was wrong.

"Kyrah, I've known you forever. I know something is wrong. What is it?" Kaelin pressed.

Finally, the dam burst. I started sobbing uncontrollably. Between the tears, I managed to say, "I'm not happy. I feel so lonely."

"What do you mean you're lonely?" Kaelin asked. "How can you be lonely? I'm here with you all day. We're never apart unless you go to your parents' house. And while you're there, you have your mom and your sisters. How can you possibly be lonely?"

"I don't know, but I am," I said. "I don't know what's wrong with me, but I know that I'm not happy." We talked for a long time, but I still could not articulate the real problem. What I wish I could have said was that I felt like he put work over me and my needs. I felt like Kaelin was there, but that he wasn't *really* there. And I needed him.

However, our problems weren't all on him. I wish I'd known at that time that the way I reacted to this huge upheaval in my life was not going to be unique. I have since learned that I am not a person who does well with change. I should have clued in to this fact by the way I live day to day. I eat the same food every day at the same time and I go to the same park and I never see the need to try anything new. I find comfort in repetition and habit, but with a new marriage in a new apartment, I had no repetition and no familiar habits to fall back on. I found myself completely out of my comfort zone, which is what sent me running back to my mom. Life there was no different than it had been when I could not wait to leave, but at least it was familiar, and that's what I craved: familiarity. I'm not sure there was anything Kaelin could have done at the time to change any of this. Even if he'd been the most sensitive, caring, affectionate husband any girl could have dreamed of, I would still have wrestled with much of what I was feeling because it welled up from within me.

I wish I could have said all of this, but instead I told him I was lonely.

KAELIN:

I really didn't know what was going on with Kyrah. I thought we were communicating. When I sensed something was wrong, I asked her about it. She always told me everything was good, and I believed her—until the night the dam burst.

That night actually began the night before. I could tell Kyrah was upset, but when I asked what was wrong, she gave me her standard answer:

"Nothing." The next morning, whatever was on her mind the night before had grown even bigger. "What's wrong, Kyrah?" I asked. "What's bothering you?"

"Nothing. I'm fine," she said, but that was pretty much all she said to me all morning. After a little while, she said, "I'm going over to my mom's."

Surprise, surprise, I thought, but I said, "Okay. But when you get home, I need you. We need to plan and shoot our videos for next week."

"Okay," she said on her way out. I wasn't kidding about needing her help. The sooner she came home, the better. But she was gone all day.

She was always gone all day. I found myself alone constantly, and increasingly frustrated. That motivated me to start my own YouTube channel that I could work on without needing her. It was an instant success, but even with the extra workload, some days I had too much time alone and some old habits from my past came creeping back in. I found a way to justify it to myself. My wife was always gone, and what was a man supposed to do? I felt a little guilty, but not enough to talk to Kyrah about what was happening because to do that would mean having a big conversation about my past and I saw no need to open up that can of worms. That past was way past, predating my relationship with Kyrah—at least most of it did. Besides, that past had nothing to do with our present difficulties. I had no idea what was causing those. How could I if Kyrah never opened up about them to me?

When Kyrah finally came home this particular day, she was still visibly upset with me. I knew this couldn't go on much longer. I pressed her. "You have to tell me what's wrong, Kyrah, because this is driving me crazy."

And that's when the dam burst. She told me she was not happy and that she was lonely. Her words hit me hard. "Why?" I asked.

"I don't know," she said as she began to cry harder.

"Is that why you spend so much time at your mom's house?" I asked.

"Yeah. Probably. I don't know. It's just I'm here in this apartment with no one around and I just can't take it. That's why I go to my mom's. I have her there, and my sisters."

"But I'm here," I said.

Kyrah just cried in response.

In that moment, I heard my wife's words, but I did not hear her. I did not understand what she was really saying to me. Both of us were having trouble adjusting to married life. That much was obvious to me. For me, I convinced myself that the only thing I was really struggling with was figuring out how to make a completely different approach to our channel work while keeping our ship afloat financially. I convinced myself that I was supposed to make sure we had money coming in and if I did that, my job here was mostly done. What I did not want to recognize was how my telling myself this also fed my natural tendency toward becoming a workaholic. Instead, I told myself that I had a strong work ethic. Now that our source of income had suddenly become precarious, I needed that work ethic more than ever. I told myself that it was the uncertainty about our work and our channel that I was having trouble adjusting to—not married life. A couple more years and a cross-country move had to happen before I finally admitted the truth to myself.

However, in this moment in our apartment with Kyrah crying and telling me she was lonely, I did not need to figure out how I was feeling. I needed to hear what my wife was really saying. She was telling me that she felt alone in my presence, that even though I was present physically, I was not present emotionally or spiritually. That's what my wife most needed from me. I didn't hear her then. Not fully. Not long after, we also received a surprise that convinced me she'd never be lonely again, not for at least eighteen years: we were going to have a baby!

14

Getting on the Same Team

KYRAH:

For the first six months of our marriage, it felt like Kaelin and I were on opposing teams fighting to come together as one. When we did our pranks, our viewers definitely divided into Team Kaelin and Team Kyrah, and now we had as well. But the moment the doctor told us that we were having a baby, we both knew without saying a word that we had to get on the same team before this baby arrived. It turned out to be harder than I expected.

I was so excited to be pregnant. And then one morning a wave of nausea washed over me the moment I climbed out of bed. I knew what was about to hit me, so I rushed to the bathroom. After throwing up, I thought to myself, *Okay, whatever was making me feel bad is now out of my system. I'll be fine now.* But I was not fine. I could hardly move without nearly throwing up again. I climbed back into bed and waited to feel better, but I never did. I had to lie very still to keep the nausea from hitting me. However, if I tried to get up, I'd lose whatever I'd eaten.

The next day was the same, as was the next and the next and the next for pretty much the first three months of my pregnancy. I'm not sure why they call this "morning sickness" because for me it always lasted longer than the morning. Most days, I did not start to feel like myself until six or seven in the evening.

I wish I could say Kaelin was the perfect, understanding, supportive husband who attended to my every need and massaged my feet and took great care of me. Kaelin and I were still only twenty when I found out I was pregnant, and it showed in how he responded to my morning sickness. Instead of acting with his heart, he reacted with logic. Or, as I called it at the time, like trash.

KAELIN:

I am embarrassed to even include this story in this book, and before you decide you think I'm the biggest jerk to ever walk the earth, please understand that I was wrong and insensitive and toxic, basically the worst husband in the world at that time. I was also twenty and thought I knew it all, even how morning sickness affects women.

I got up early the first day Kyrah became ill, like I did almost every day, and had already started working on the plans for that day's video shoot. After a few hours, there was still no Kyrah. I found her in bed lying in the same position she had been in hours earlier. Kyrah wasn't a morning person at the time, but it was unlike her to drag out getting up this long.

"Hey, are you okay?" I asked.

"I feel nauseous. I've been throwing up all day...," she said. Before she could finish that sentence, she was struggling to the bathroom again.

I caught her and helped her into the bathroom and then helped her back to bed afterward. So far, so good.

The same thing continued to happen until Kyrah decided that the only way to keep from throwing up every morning was to stay put. In bed. All day. The first couple of times she told me this, I said, "Okay. Let me know when you feel better." However, the more I thought about Kyrah lying in bed all day while I did all the work, the more it ate at me. Logic told me that women have been having babies for millennia without the luxury of staying in bed through the entire pregnancy. I had worked with women at the credit union who'd had babies. They'd managed to get out of bed and come in to work a full day, standing up until right before their babies were born. I was sure they all felt the same way, but pushed themselves and got through it. *Why can't Kyrah? What makes her morning sickness so much worse that she can't function?* I considered the possibility that her symptoms were worse than every other woman who has had a baby, but it didn't add up. The way I saw it, there was really only one conclusion to draw: Kyrah was using her pregnancy as an excuse not to work. I wondered if she even had such intense morning sickness or if she was playing it up.

Me thinking all of this was awful enough. And yes, I knew it was horrible and awful and stupid. But I found a way to make it even worse. I told Kyrah exactly what I was thinking.

KYRAH:

"You think I'm doing what?!" I said to Kaelin when he informed me that he thought my morning sickness was made up.

"Maybe made up is the wrong word. But I can't see how morning sickness keeps you from working at *all*. You didn't want to get out of bed before. This seems to be a very convenient excuse," he said.

I had absolutely no words for him.

"I've looked up pregnancy symptoms and I know they are strong, but we *have* to work," Kaelin went on. "I think maybe you have some of the placebo effect; since you're always researching pregnancy symptoms, you think you have everything you've read about and start feeling the symptoms. I know it's gotta be tough, but can you push through?"

"You're serious," I said, seething.

"Yes," he said.

I stared a hole through Kaelin for a very long time. Finally, I said, "I am not getting out of this bed and I DO NOT feel guilty about it. Every time I stand up, I THROW UP."

Kaelin left the room, and it was a good thing he did. I lay there, flabbergasted. Who says that? I mean, what husband tells his wife she's exaggerating morning sickness when she's carrying *their* child? I don't think I'd ever been so mad at Kaelin. When we were dating, I always had him on a pedestal as this loving, caring guy. Now I could only think of one word to describe him: trash. I'd married a trash guy who basically called me a liar for having morning sickness.

When I finally did feel well enough to get out of bed, I didn't stick around. I went to my mom's house. She saw the steam pouring out of my ears. Before she asked what the matter was, I vented. I told her everything Kaelin had said. My mom was about ready to go over to our apartment and dismantle Kaelin for me.

My mom didn't do it that day, but the next time she saw Kaelin, she went off on him. The two of us went over to see my parents, and no sooner had Kaelin walked in than my mom said, "You think morning sickness is a placebo effect. What is wrong with you? How could you say that to her?!"

KAELIN:

When Kyrah's mom went off on me, I knew I deserved it, but I also looked over at Kyrah and thought, *Wait. Whoa. How does your mom even know about this?* She hadn't been at our apartment when we'd had this conversation, and I certainly hadn't repeated it to her. Kyrah's mom also didn't know the context of my frustration with Kyrah not even wanting to work much before she was pregnant. And her mother also did not understand the pressure we were under with the changes to our channel. After we announced the end of Kaelin and Kyrah as our audience knew us, we phased out our prank videos completely. Just as I'd feared, we lost a big part of our audience. But, at the same time, our numbers for engagement went up. That meant our new audience responded in much stronger ways than our old audience ever did, which helped us with brand deals and advertising. The problem was our subscribers tuned in to our channel to see Kaelin AND Kyrah. We had to have both of us on our channel, not just me, especially at this crucial transition time from our old approach to our new one.

I could have explained all of this to Kyrah's mom and made my case for why I was trying to encourage Kyrah to push through her morning sickness, but I didn't feel I needed to explain anything to her. Kyrah knew where I was coming from, so I took the heat and never brought it up with her again. But having Kyrah's mom jump on me over something Kyrah and I talked about in private revealed a much larger problem to me. I'm not excusing what I said to Kyrah, but I really thought this was something the two of us needed to work out together. I wanted Kyrah to talk to me when something was bothering her, not vent to her mother.

A couple days later, Kyrah was out of bed and slumped on the couch, watching television. I walked in, but she barely acknowledged me. *Uh-oh*, I thought. "What's wrong?" I asked.

"Nothing."

"It seems like something is bothering you," I pressed.

"Nothing."

I kept pressing and pressing and pressing until I realized that the more I asked Kyrah what was wrong, the worse I was making her feel. She seemed exhausted…by my *words*. A little light came on. Her mom had always suggested that sometimes I should just give Kyrah room to breathe, but I felt we needed to address any issues that came up immediately. I'm pretty confrontational, so staying quiet isn't my strong suit. When we were dating, we'd talk on the phone for hours, with me doing most of the talking. Once we moved in together, my talking wasn't the only thing draining her. If she left shoes or food out, I nagged and reminded her that every-thing has a place and everything should be returned to its place after being used. I literally always had something to say about *everything*. My words didn't help pull us together. Instead, I saw me pushing her further away.

When the light came on, I shut up.

I stopped nitpicking over little things in the apartment, and I stopped interrogating her over how she was feeling when she looked sad. I shut my mouth and said nothing. And I waited. The first day, nothing. Kyrah didn't say anything to me about whatever was on her mind. The next day, nothing again. I kept quiet, which was a lot harder than I'd expected it to be. I literally had to bite my tongue. Again, my difficulty in keeping my mouth shut showed me that I was more controlling than I thought I was and much more than I'd ever wanted to be.

Finally, after a few days of giving Kyrah space, we started talking in a more productive way. Both of us realized that with a baby on the way, we had to get on the same team and fast. We needed to get committed and get to work. And most of the work I needed to do was inside myself. As we have both written before, marriage exposes you. It reveals parts of yourself that you didn't know were there, and not in a good way. We had less than nine months to work through those hard parts of ourselves. Unfortunately, it's hard to work on a part of you hiding in your blind spot.

KYRAH:

When my mom took up for me, it felt both right and wrong at the same time. I was glad Kaelin finally knew how I felt. But I couldn't stop asking myself, *Why didn't I tell him?* What was keeping me from actually express-ing myself to my husband? Rather than talk about what was bothering me, I found it easier to blame Kaelin for everything I didn't like about my life. Work was the easiest place to become the victim and make Kaelin out to be the bad guy. Even though he always said the channel was ours, from the start I looked at it as his. In my mind, he was the boss and I worked for him, which meant he shouldered all the responsibilities and I got to act like a frequently disgruntled employee. Everything was always his fault, and I was the innocent victim. Going over to my mom's house fed the victim inside of me. She always took my side; she always blamed Kaelin; she always showered me with sympathy. Again, it felt good, but it wasn't healthy. It fueled my victim's mind-set and placed Kaelin and me in opposite corners, fighting against each other rather than working toward one common goal. If we kept this up, we weren't going to make it.

We had a baby on the way. Not making it was not an option. More than that, I loved Kaelin and I wanted the two of us to have a strong, successful marriage. Claiming the role of the victim was not going to make that happen. I needed to change. I also needed to stop floating along. I wasted so much time mindlessly watching television. I was sick of that. I had to get my stuff together and start growing and changing and becoming the wife and mom I needed to be.

The first step seemed pretty obvious. I opened up and started talking to Kaelin about how I felt. Even though we loved Jesus, since we'd gotten married, we'd been very lax about growing in our relationship with Him. I hardly read my Bible, and we were never together with other Christians. We had to change that. Since we were first married, we'd bounced back and forth between Kaelin's dad's church and my church, never really committing to either. "We need to go to one church and do that consistently," Kaelin said.

"Yeah, I agree," I said. I can't tell you how relieved I felt. I knew if I were going to grow in my relationship with Him, I'd need to surround myself with people who loved Him and made Him a priority in their lives.

KAELIN:

The Sunday after we decided to go all in attending one church, we had the bright idea of going to the early service. We'd never attended that service before. When we walked in, we stuck out like a sore thumb. Everyone else in this service was white and old. If I'd wanted to go someplace the exact opposite of my dad's church, we were there. The early service was sort of like the early-bird special at a restaurant and served basically the same crowd. However, the music and the message were the same as the later service, which gave everything a familiar feel. By the time the service was over, I had nearly forgotten we were the only two people there who were under fifty.

Kyrah must have been moved by the message, because as soon as we walked out of the service, she went over to a booth and signed us up for a small group. I kind of panicked. My mind raced. *My dad always warned me about going to a small group Bible study away from the church building... This is something I should be leading...I haven't had a chance to even vet this place and go over its statement of faith...I don't know who they are connected to. They say they're nondenominational but they're going to show us who they really are and try to convert us to whatever denomination they're really a part of.* I kicked into full-on skeptic mode. I tried to stop Kyrah before it was too late. "Don't you think this is something we need to discuss?" I asked.

"Nope," she replied.

"What...," I said.

"We need friends, Kaelin—married friends. Since we got married, I hardly see Daja, and Brandon has moved off for college. We need to connect with people, and I think this is a good way to do it."

"I think you're right," I said.

The following Thursday, the two of us drove to a stranger's house to hang out with people I did not know and wasn't sure I could trust. To be honest, our first impression didn't make me feel any more confident.

We knocked on the door, and who answers but a middle-aged white couple—not exactly people I assumed we could relate to. Brandi and Trevor welcomed us into their home, and honestly, they couldn't have been any nicer. We sat down and started some small talk when their dog came in and started jumping on us and trying to lick me. "Whoa, whoa, whoa," I said. Trevor apologized and told the dog to get down. I thought I might as well be completely up front, so I told him, "I know we just met, but I am a real honest guy and I have to tell you that I am not exactly a pet person. I don't like animals."

I half expected this to put Trevor and Brandi off. After all, a lot of people see themselves as pet parents, not dog owners. If you don't like the dog, you don't like them—that's the vibe I get from a lot of people. But not these people. "My bad, man," Trevor said. "I'll get her out of here," and he did without a trace of resentment.

Other people started arriving. One couple, Grant and Tabitha, was Mexican, and it made me happy to see a little color mixed into the group beyond Kyrah and me. Everyone was basically new to the group, which made the first night a little less awkward. We discovered that Brandi and Trevor had only recently become Christians. When they started following Jesus, they lost a lot of their old friends. Over the next several weeks and months, they ended up becoming some of our closest friends. Thanks to our small group, my church became something more than a church: it now felt like home.

Not only did we get involved in a small group, but we also signed up for a class called Financial Peace University by Dave Ramsey. As soon as I saw the class, I told Kyrah, "We have to take this." My motives weren't exactly the purest of pure. Kyrah and I had never been on the same page financially. Of course, I thought getting on the same page meant Kyrah coming around to see things my way. After all, I had long ago adopted the Ramsey approach of keeping a very tight, detailed budget. Kyrah had always been a free spirit when it came to money. Our differences caused conflict, especially when the holidays rolled around and Kyrah wanted to go shopping for everyone but I kept constantly replying, "But it's not in the budget!"

"Why not? We have the money!" Kyrah usually replied. I'd always heard that couples argued about money, but I'd always assumed that was because they didn't have enough of it to cover their expenses. That wasn't a problem for us, but we still had issues.

With FPU, I saw the chance for Kyrah to see the light and come around to my way of thinking. Boy, was I wrong. Instead of Kyrah having a target on her back, I discovered I was the one who needed a complete change in my way of thinking. Rather than condemning the free-spirited spender, FPU showed me that the spender and the saver are two personality types with different gifts, and neither is more valuable than the other. The two need to come together as one team of partners whose unique outlooks and gifts must work together for the team to function at its highest level. Before FPU, I'd plan the budget, then spend hours trying to convince Kyrah to stick to it. In these classes, we discovered that it's best if the planners draft the budget, then allow the free spirit to adjust it. After going through FPU, my hours-long budget lectures turned into the two of us having a productive fifteen-minute conversation about our finances. We became one team rather than two individuals fighting for their own way.

It didn't take me long to realize that more than my approach to finances needed to change. I began to see how I spent more time talking *at* my wife instead of talking *with* her. The difference is huge. We had to get to the point of talking together, of communicating and giving and compromising, if we were ever going to get on the same team. I'd never expected a class on getting your finances in order to show me so much more.

The classes helped us start communicating. They weren't some sort of magic pill that solved everything all at once. If you haven't picked up on it yet, I'll let you in on the secret of growing a marriage: Everything takes time. Lots and lots of time. You'll have breakthrough moments along the way, and those are great. But even when the breakthrough moments arrive, you have to learn from them and build on them. Often, they come when you least expect it.

Kyrah and I continued preparing for the baby's arrival. December rolled around, and we realized this was going to be our last Christmas with just the two of us. We should have enjoyed it, and I wanted to, but one of those breakthrough moments for us as a couple hit and absolutely blindsided me. I keep saying that marriage brings out things about yourself you never realized were there. That's what this moment did to me, and what I discovered was very, very ugly.

Eight months had passed since we'd changed our channel's content from childish pranks to inviting people to come in and do life together with us. I'd been nervous about the change when we started, but the new business model proved to be even more successful financially, and with far less work. Kyrah and I started the process of buying a house and getting everything ready for our new baby. Life was good.

But then we hit a snag in the form of a glitch in the algorithm on You-Tube. All of a sudden, we couldn't put ads on our channel, which meant that no matter how many views we had, we didn't receive any money from them. As soon as I noticed the problem, I contacted the YouTube technical team. They assured me they'd get it fixed, but in a place the size of You-Tube, problems with one little channel out of millions don't get fixed in a day. I spent a lot of time going back and forth with the tech team as they tried to figure out what the problem might be. All the while, days kept going by, and we lost more and more money. The glitch by itself was bad enough, but the timing could not have been worse. Since we are a family-friendly channel, we have premium ads, and the December shopping season is the prime time for those ads.

A week went by. The tech team still didn't know what the problem was. We still posted new content because if we stopped posting, we risked losing the high engagement of our audience. Our pregnancy journey proved to be one of the most popular series of videos we'd ever done. Our audience was engaged, which was great. But we were doing our channel for free, which was not. And it wasn't like we could recover the money later. No ads meant no ad income until we were able to monetize again. No one knew when that might be.

After another week of no ads, we stopped posting pregnancy videos, and shortly after, we stopped posting new content altogether. It's hard to put your heart and soul into your work when you know you won't get paid for it. Another week went by. And another. I really started to worry. Then the calendar flipped from December to January. We'd lost tens of thousands of dollars. I felt sick, but there was nothing I could do about it. I pulled myself together and told myself that we'd be okay. The problem couldn't last much longer.

But it did. The glitch took a month and a half to fix. The longer it went on, the less incentive I felt to do anything with our channel. Usually I was the one telling Kyrah we needed to get to work. Now she said to me, "Aren't we going to post anything new?"

"I guess we could, but without any ad income, why bother?" I said.

"Did you just hear yourself?" Kyrah said.

Unfortunately, I had. My words told me that I loved money. I didn't just love it. Money had become my idol. For years, I'd made YouTube videos for free when it seemed like no one was watching. Now here I was feeling sorry for myself, taking for granted and neglecting the very audience that supported me and my family. I justified my drive for money to myself by saying I needed to provide for my family, but we had plenty of money in the bank and plenty of money coming in through endorsement and merchandise sales to get through these weeks without ad income. Yet, my attitude nosedived when *more* money stopped coming in. What was wrong with me?

That realization caused me to step back and look at our first year of marriage through a different lens. Yes, we'd built an incredible brand of which I was very proud. But at what cost? I slowly started to see the correlation between my love of money and Kyrah's loneliness. My love of money had turned me into a workaholic who was emotionally absent from the woman to whom I'd pledged my life. I had gotten lost in the sauce. Our platform and monetary success had grown so quickly that I didn't have time to develop the character necessary to steward it well. I had to come clean with Kyrah. I had to put work in its proper place, and that place was not in front of my wife. In the spirit of opportunism and recognizing YouTube money was not normal, my dad had once told me that I needed to make all the money I could while I could. All the money in the world didn't matter if it cost me my marriage.

In the midst of this moment of self-awareness, another thought hit me like a ton of bricks. I thought about this child who was on the way. God forbid that I raise him or her to be just like me. All my life, I'd had this plan of where I wanted to go and what I wanted to do and what I wanted to be. In this moment I realized that what I really wanted was to be the kind of man my children would grow up and want to be like. I wasn't there yet. Not even close.

15

From the Highest of Highs to the Lowest of Lows

KYRAH:

I dozed off in the recliner in the baby's room, enjoying what I didn't know was my last night with a baby in my womb. A sharp stomach cramp pulled me out of my catnap around eight. I sat up for a moment and thought, *Could this be it?* When the pain went away as quickly as it had come, I wrote it off as my imagination. Today, May 27, was my due date. Babies never come right on their due date.

But then another cramp hit. The second pain wasn't nearly as easy to dismiss as the first. Even so, it was probably nothing more than Braxton Hicks, or practice contractions. There's no way I had actually gone into labor. Was there?

I FaceTimed my mom. "I'm having some serious stomach cramps. This can't be labor, can it?"

"How bad are they?" she asked.

"It woke me up from a nap," I said.

My dad must've heard me. "If they get to the point where you can't talk through them, you'll know it's the real thing," he said.

My mom and I stayed on the phone for probably an hour while I organized all of the baby clothes and diapers and made sure the nursery was as ready as possible for our baby boy. We'd discovered the baby's gender during an ultrasound appointment when I was at sixteen weeks. When I first discovered I was pregnant, I thought for sure I'd have a girl. I imagined the two of us doing all sorts of girly things together, like getting our nails done or taking her to cheer competitions. Over the past twenty-four weeks, I'd prepared myself for superhero parties and football games and everything else that comes with having a little boy.

My wait felt like it was about to come to an end. Over the course of the hour of talking to my mom on the phone, my cramping went from mild contractions into pangs I didn't want to talk through. However, they weren't frequent enough to pack up and head to the hospital.

A bit later Kaelin came home from playing basketball. As soon as he walked in, I told him, "The baby is coming!"

"What? Really?! Do we need to go to the hospital?" he said, excited.

"The pains aren't close enough together yet. If we go now, they'll just send us home. But the baby is coming. I bet we have him in the middle of the night," I said.

"So, what do we do for now?" Kaelin asked.

"I guess we try to get some sleep until it's time."

We went to bed, and Kaelin might have gone to sleep, but I didn't. My stomach cramps turned into back labor, which kept me awake all night. As soon as I saw the sun coming up, the contractions were finally close enough together that I knew it was time to head to the hospital. I hopped out of bed and straight into the shower to get ready for my labor and delivery. After I got out of the shower and got dressed, I woke Kaelin up. "It is Time! To! Go!" I said.

"Okay, okay," he said, and started getting ready.

While Kaelin got ready, I started to panic internally a bit, thinking I might have labored at home too long and might accidentally have the baby in our house. Before checking into the hospital, we drove to have breakfast at the Mexican grill Kaelin used to work at in high school. It had become one of our favorite Mexican food spots. I struggled to keep my composure because my contractions were getting too intense. I had been in labor for twelve hours at this point, and my contractions were getting closer and closer together. "Kaelin, I think we need to go now."

We quickly wrapped up our breakfast and drove to the hospital. They took me to the triage area to check how dilated I was before they fully admitted me. Even though I had labored a while before getting to the hospital, I felt a great deal of peace. I wasn't really that nervous. I was just ready to hold my baby in my arms.

The nurse checked me. "You're at five centimeters," she said. "That means we need to admit you ASAP. I have to tell you that I'm a little surprised you're this far along. You seem so calm that me and all the other nurses at the front desk thought for sure we would be sending you back home."

The nursing staff moved me pretty quickly from the triage area to a room. After they put in my IV, I lay in bed for a few hours until I was seven centimeters dilated. In between labor pangs, I drifted off to sleep. However, as the pangs got closer and closer together, I knew I needed to get some rest before the hard part of the delivery, the pushing, started. I still hadn't had anything for the pain, so I decided to go ahead and ask for an epidural. Perhaps I could get a little sleep before our baby made his grand arrival. A few minutes later, my nurse gave me an epidural while Kaelin held my hands.

When we'd arrived at the hospital in the morning, I'd thought for sure we'd have our baby in our arms before lunch, or before dinner at the latest. We'd already decided to name him Karter. Kaelin came up with the name. Since both of us have names that start with K, having our baby's name do the same made sense. At first, I wasn't completely sold on the name. Today, I can't imagine him being called anything else.

All through my labor process, my doctor came in to check me regularly. The labor dragged on. Finally, at nine in the evening—more than twenty-four hours since my first pain hit—my doctor checked me again and told me what I'd been waiting to hear: time to start pushing. However, because of the epidural and other pain medication they had given me throughout the day, I couldn't feel anything besides my face, neck, and arms. My entire lower body and stomach was overly numb from the epidural.

When the next contraction came, I pushed as hard as I could. And then on the next. And the next. And the next. And the next. Three hours later, I was still pushing. Even though my labor had been long, it had gone by really smoothly. Not this. No matter how much I pushed, it seemed our baby was no closer to coming out. They turned my epidural completely off, but that didn't help. They gave me a fourth-degree episiotomy, but still I kept pushing to no avail. Finally, the doctor made the call to use a vacuum to get the baby out. Twenty-eight hours after my first labor pain woke me up in the recliner, Karter was finally delivered. I was so exhausted that I didn't even have the strength to hold him. Both Karter and I had fevers. I felt like I was on fire, which raised a bit of an alarm in the delivery room. After placing Karter in my arms for just a split second, they whisked him off to the NICU because of the complications during his delivery. Kaelin went with him. I delivered my placenta, and my doctor spent an hour stitching me up.

The four hours of pushing were by far the most difficult thing I had ever done in my life. I had never wanted to give up so badly and cry to my husband that something was too hard. The trauma that my body endured, the blood, sweat, and tears that I endured bringing my firstborn into the world—it was overwhelming, to put it simply. However, in spite of all the trauma, when they brought Karter back to me after a brief one-hour stay in the NICU, all the pain and trauma and everything else were worth it. My fever had broken and my strength had returned. Holding my baby boy in my arms for the first time was the greatest feeling I'd ever experienced.

The first sign that we might have more trouble came when I tried to nurse Karter for the first time. It was extremely painful. After all of the blogs I'd read, I thought I was prepared for everything. The nurses told me not to worry, that it usually takes a few days for you and the baby to get the hang of it. "Now don't you give it a thought," they said. "Everything will be fine. Just let the baby nurse."

But nursing wasn't fine. Breastfeeding proved to be unbelievably painful and time-consuming and draining on top of all the blood draws and doctors' visits that had resulted from the complications during birth. I now had to worry about how much Karter was eating. Other moms told me to push through, that the pain only comes in the early days. Mine lasted throughout the entire time I breastfed him. I cried as I fed him, and my toes curled in agony. Most times after the feeding session we both cried, and blood dripped down my chest or into the breast pump.

My plan had always been to breastfeed him and never introduce a bottle for a few months at least, but I didn't think I'd be able to keep this up. Even thinking that way made me feel like a failure as a mom. Kaelin's mom had six kids and had breastfed them all. My sisters-in-law all breastfed their kids. One of my friends had a baby around the same time Karter was born. She didn't have any problems breastfeeding her baby. Why couldn't I push through? I felt so inadequate, like I wasn't strong enough to do the most basic thing any mom does for her child.

After five days I finally gave up, and we switched Karter to formula.

The decision nearly killed me. I now know without a shadow of a doubt that I made the right decision for my son, but at the time, I felt guilty and inadequate, like I was the worst mom in the world. Kaelin helped me get through it. "Kyrah," he said, "it doesn't matter what your mom did or what my mom did. All that matters is what is best for you and for Karter. You've been through enough already, and he deserves a mom who is happy to care for him. If that means giving him formula instead of breastfeeding him, big deal. We'll do whatever we need to do." I couldn't have made this difficult decision without his support.

Even so, I still felt waves of inadequacy over not breastfeeding, which added to what I now realize might have been postpartum depression and anxiety. After having a baby, your hormones are so out of whack that you don't feel like yourself at all. Yet what I experienced went deeper than that. I felt so down, so detached at times. I was also exhausted. Karter woke up hungry every couple of hours, so I never slept more than two hours at a time. His cries made me sweat profusely and my heart race. We tried feeding him, rocking him, and bouncing him, yet he kept crying for hours on end. When he finally stopped crying and went to sleep, Kaelin and I looked at each other and asked, "What have we gotten ourselves into? We are in waaaaaaaayyyyyyy over our heads. Why did we think having a baby so soon after getting married was a good idea?" People also weighed in with their unsolicited baby "advice" on social media, which didn't help at all. Many tried to shame us for having a baby so soon, something that came up again when I got pregnant with our second son, Kaiser, ten months later.

Between the constant crying, the inability to breastfeed, the battle with depression and anxiety, and serious sleep deprivation, I found myself starting to panic. We had just moved into a new house with all new furniture and had replaced Kaelin's beat-up, old $700 car with my dream car, a Jeep Grand Cherokee. It had felt like a fresh start, especially when Karter came along two weeks later. But all of a sudden, I didn't want a fresh start.

After one particularly rough day where it seemed that Karter never stopped crying, I wanted to run away and claw my way back to our old apartment and old furniture and old car and old life. I could not cope with the life I now had. I kept wondering why no one had warned me that this could happen. My mother had had children young. Why hadn't she told me about the sleep deprivation and the constant crying? Kaelin's mom had six kids, but she'd never opened up about how difficult the first few weeks can be. And neither of them jumped in much to stay with us and help us through these difficult first few weeks. My mom and dad watched Karter a few times, but they still had three kids at home and my dad still worked out of town for days at a time. Kaelin's mom did spend one night with us, but she had prior commitments to the church. I guess I assumed they'd come to our rescue. But they didn't.

With little help from the outside, Kaelin and I did our best to get through those rough first few months on our own. The two of us decided that there was no sense in both of us getting up through the night with Karter, so I did nights and Kaelin took the mornings and early afternoons. The plan seemed easy enough, but like most things early in our marriage, we took it to levels we shouldn't have. We thought that everything needed to be fifty-fifty. If Kaelin changed Karter's last diaper, I needed to change the next one. If Kaelin got four hours of sleep, I needed four hours of sleep and not a minute less. Then we started to retaliate against each other. If I made the last bottle, Kaelin needed to make the next one. If I was up in the middle of the night, Kaelin needed to do something in order to make it even. We both always felt like we were doing more than the other person, and it all got ugly and selfish.

I'm not proud of how we acted. Neither of us is. I think the petty, tit-for-tat score-keeping came out of the biggest thing we kept score of: who got to sleep. Neither one of us ever got enough sleep. What little sleep we did get we guarded like it was pure gold. I think we fought over sleep more than anything else. Worse, I told my mom about it, which is the last thing any couple should do when they find themselves pulling in different directions rather than working on the same team. My mom actually gave us some really good advice. She told me that since Kaelin and I both made this baby and we both love this baby, both of us needed to take care of this baby and do what is best for him without worrying about what the other did or did not do. Caring for a child is not a fifty-fifty but a one hundred–one hundred proposition. That was the best advice she'd ever given me. I only wish I'd followed it from the start.

Everything came to a head one afternoon when Kaelin's shift with Karter had ended. I woke up to several texts from one of our managers about a document she needed from me that day. I'd started on it, but I hadn't finished. Our manager needed it right away. I went into the family room and told Kaelin, "I need to go work for a while, so you'll need to watch Karter until I'm done."

Kaelin shook his head. "I'm too exhausted. I've been up for eight hours. I have to get some sleep. You can take care of that after I get up." He then walked into our bedroom and shut the door behind him.

I sat there and stewed for a while. Kaelin had been on me constantly about needing me to work more. Now that I was actually working, he went to take a nap and left me with the baby! With how fussy Karter was, I couldn't work and watch the baby. Besides, by the time Kaelin got up, it would be my turn to sleep. I'd spent the night before sitting in the rocking chair while he'd had all night to sleep peacefully in our bed. But he hadn't taken advantage of his time. I'd heard him up and about until well after midnight. That's why he was so tired now. He should have slept when he'd had the chance. I knew he could stay up longer now and let me get my work done!

As if on cue, as my frustration peaked, Karter started crying. I went from frustrated to angry. I had work I had to do, and I couldn't do it with a fussy baby. I then picked up Karter in his carrier, took him into the room where Kaelin was trying to sleep, set Karter down, and walked out.

A few minutes later, Kaelin came back with Karter. Without saying a word, he set the baby down next to me, then walked back into our room and closed the door. I turned around and took Karter back in to Kaelin. We went back and forth like this a couple of times before Kaelin locked the bedroom door after depositing the baby with me. Locks don't work when someone else has the key, and I had the key. I unlocked the door and placed Karter back in with Kaelin.

"You have to let me sleep," Kaelin said.

"You had all night to sleep, but you stayed up until one in the morning. You should have slept then," I said.

"I stayed up doing the work that allows you to take a break," he snapped back.

"Yeah right. You were probably playing video games!" I snapped right back at him.

We kept arguing like this for a while until finally Kaelin said, "If you don't let me sleep, I'm going to leave." Before I could say anything, he jumped out of bed, went into the bathroom, and started taking a shower. This really just set me off. I couldn't put the baby in the shower, but I could make sure Kaelin couldn't leave. I went into the other room and grabbed his car keys out of our junk drawer and started looking for a place to hide them. A month or so earlier, I'd misplaced my keys and still hadn't been able to find them. That made Kaelin's set our only set.

As I wandered around, looking for the perfect place to hide his keys, Karter started crying again. I stuffed the keys under my arm and went into the living room and picked him up. I was still trying to soothe Karter when Kaelin entered the hallway and walked right past me to the junk drawer. But his keys weren't there. He rushed back down the hall, where he found me holding Karter and acting clueless. It was a standoff.

"Where are my keys?" he asked.

"I don't know," I lied.

Kaelin knew I was lying. "What did you do with my keys?" he asked accusingly.

"I don't know!" I lied again.

Kaelin walked over close to me. "Kyrah. Where are my keys?"

"You aren't going anywhere," I said. I tried to sidestep and walk past him, but he mirrored my movement and blocked my path.

Kaelin grasped the sides of my shoulders, which made me back up into a cabinet. My tailbone pressed up against it as Kaelin steadied me squarely in front of him. Looking deep into my eyes, he demanded, "Give me my keys."

"Get out of my face," I yelled. Kaelin repeated himself and moved closer. I hated being controlled. "Let go of me!" I screamed. I grew angrier and angrier because he refused to listen to me. My vision blurred. The next thing I knew, my hand was burning hot. I didn't know what'd just happened. CLACK! Kaelin's keys slid from under my armpit and crashed onto the floor. It wasn't until Kaelin jumped back, holding his face where I had slapped him as hard as I could, that I realized what I had done. We stared at each other for a moment, both of us in shock.

Kaelin reacted first by snatching his keys from the ground. Then he walked back over to me and calmly took Karter out of my arms. "You are out of control," he said. He turned and went back into the living room and put Karter into his carrier.

"What are you doing?" I yelled as Kaelin moved around the room, gathering things into Karter's diaper bag. Kaelin didn't answer. "Are you leaving? You can't leave," I said again.

Still no answer as he picked the baby up and headed toward the garage.

I looked around. I was still in my pajamas, but I could not let him leave with the baby and without me. Without thinking, I ran out and jumped in our car as Kaelin was about to pull out of the garage. He didn't say a word. He pulled out of the garage and started driving. A few minutes later, he pulled into the parking lot of The Marketplace. Even though there were spots with shade on the far ends of the parking lot, Kaelin parked in the sunniest spot there was. It was mid-August, in Bakersfield, where summer temperatures hit triple digits before noon every day and stay that way well after the sun goes down. Kaelin took Karter and went into a store. I couldn't follow them, not barefoot in my bathrobe.

As I sat baking in the car, my door cracked open for air, I started to cool down emotionally. The reality of what had happened at the house hit me. I could not believe I'd slapped my husband. I'd never thought I could ever do something like this. Until now. Now I knew it was deep inside of me, and that thought scared me to death. I'd always thought I was this very sweet, slow-to-anger, Jesus-loving girl who could never in a million years do something like this. But I had, and it horrified me.

By the time Kaelin came back out to the car, I felt so guilty. I was also a little angry that he'd parked in the hottest place he could find in the hottest month of the year in the hottest place on earth. When Kaelin got back in the car, I started trying to talk about what had happened, but he ignored me. He then drove to Walmart and parked once again in the sunniest spot. When he finally returned to the car, we drove in silence back to our house. The whole time, I kept saying, "Kaelin, we need to talk about what just happened." But he stayed silent like he hadn't heard me.

He pulled the car back into the garage of our house. He went to take the baby out. I got out of the car and went into the house. The next thing I knew, I heard the garage door open. I looked out. Kaelin and Karter were gone. I knew he wasn't *gone* gone, but gone for now. I sat in our house, alone, in tears for a long time. Still, Kaelin did not come back. I called his mom and asked if he was there. He wasn't. Later she texted me and told me that he had come over with Karter. I didn't go over, but instead waited.

Time dragged by. I was broken. I took out my Bible and my journal and began pouring out my heart to God. The ugliness of what came spilling out of me horrified me. I could make excuses. I could blame the sleep deprivation and the postpartum depression, but ultimately, what I could not get away from was that when I was pushed hard enough, the worst in me came spilling out. The slap was in me. That degree of anger came from inside of me. And if it came out once, it could come out again. I couldn't live with myself if it did, and I knew my marriage could not survive it.

"Oh, God, I repent, I plead with you to change me from the inside out," I prayed. Jeremiah 17:9 says, "The heart is deceitful above all things, and desperately sick; who can understand it?" I'd read that verse before, but never like this. "Desperately sick" described my heart. I needed God to give me a new heart.

Kaelin came home that evening without saying anything to me. We didn't speak for a couple of days.

Finally, we did.

The conversation went beyond a single day. Honestly, I was scared. Shortly before the altercation, we had laughed together over lunch. I had trouble believing we could go from laughter to screaming in such a short time. I'd screamed, at least. Kaelin had stayed composed the entire time. That doesn't mean he was without fault, he admitted. He knew how to push my buttons, and he did that day. But that's not an excuse for what I did. I apologized and asked for forgiveness, which Kaelin gave. He apologized as well, and I forgave him. That doesn't mean everything immediately returned to normal. We had more conversations where he made it clear that he was not going to live in an abusive marriage. Neither of us was willing to do that. The emotions we both felt took a while to completely subside. For me, the fear remained over what I saw inside of me.

However, within a few days and after more long talks, we came back together. Things were not the same as they'd been before. They haven't been the same since. Things are better. We had both seen the worst in each other—at least he'd seen it in me—and forgiveness, not resentment and bitterness, followed. Forgiveness lets go of the past and moves forward. Circling back continually to that awful day and reliving those feelings could not be an option. Real love forgives and moves beyond the past. Seeing Kaelin express this love to me is how I began to understand what true love looks like. Anyone can love another on their best day. Real love comes out on our worst.

KAELIN:

When Kyrah slapped me, I got to play the victim and reap those benefits. Clearly, she was in the wrong and I had been wronged. However, nothing is ever as simple as it seems. The slap wasn't Kyrah's best day, but it certainly wasn't mine either. I knew what I was doing as I took Karter back and forth between our bedroom and living room. I had also contributed to Kyrah's stress levels by not having the best discretion in the world over what we posted online. When she got pregnant, we were still in the process of transitioning our channel's content. We began building a new audience by candidly sharing our lives, which made documenting the pregnancy journey feel like the natural thing to do. We'd moved on from our childish pranks. We'd gotten married and grown up. Nothing said "adult" more than showing the real transition into parenthood. We started documenting everything, and our audience loved it. We could tell that the shift really struck a chord. The new content resonated so well that our audience became even more engaged, and our new community became known for its positive, affirming comments. So far, so good.

As we approached the full term of the pregnancy, the anticipation and excitement of Karter's birth led to a spike in views and retention beyond anything we had experienced before. We revisited our previous highs in month-over-month subscriber growth, views, and revenue. We even had the backing of YouTube, as they featured our content across the site. Being promoted in that way led to even more growth and validated our "family-friendly" status. That, in turn, led to more lucrative campaigns with the largest brands.

With all cylinders firing, everything was going better than I had ever anticipated. We had favor with the algorithm, an eager audience, and the top brands in the world reaching out to us. To keep feeding the beast was an easy decision. After our son's birth, we didn't skip a beat. In fact, I took it to the next level and decided to document and share every day of his first month of life. Other than the obvious lack of privacy for our growing family, the other problem that arose was something more unsettling. Since I was the primary director on the channel and Kyrah and I had the shift assignments we'd agreed to, I shot most of the footage from my perspective in the morning while Kyrah slept. As a result, our audience saw me—not both of us—caring for our baby. The comments showed that. People praised me for being so involved and hands on, but came down on Kyrah, wondering why she wasn't doing her job as a mom. Those comments fed into the struggles she already had. They also fed into the martyr complex I had about carrying most of the load of making our business a success. Throw in the sleep deprivation we both felt, along with the jealousy I felt toward Kyrah because it looked like she had a more natural connection with Karter those first few weeks than I had (and yes, that's something first-time dads go through), and you have a tinderbox that was eventually going to explode. I helped initiate that explosion when I kept pushing back as Kyrah pushed at me. The whole reason I jumped in the shower that day was because I knew she couldn't expect me to watch the baby while I was in there. And I *showered*. That shower had to have been twice as long as my usual. And while we're coming clean, yes, when she jumped into the car in her pajamas, I intentionally parked in the hottest parts of the parking lots to be petty.

So no, that wasn't my best day either. The decision I had to make after we saw the worst in each other was what to do now. Once I cooled down and Kyrah and I started talking, I was ready to move past our little hiccup. During the initial days after the incident, I ghosted her before realizing that my actions weren't helping us move on. For that, we had to lay our pride down and talk, honestly, openly, and without agendas. We both ended up taking a very long look at the baggage we'd carried into our marriage, baggage that we had to take responsibility for and that had the potential to weigh us down and destroy us if we didn't lay it aside.

Our worst day then proved to be a turning point for good. We moved past it in the sense that forgiveness flowed, and that day has become a teaching point rather than an old grievance to revisit. However, in another sense, we choose not to move past it because we do not want to forget what we are capable of when we give in to our worst instincts and pull away from each other rather than work together. In the weeks that followed, Kyrah and I became closer than we had ever been before. We had been *through* something. Overall, we both felt like we not only survived the experience but also came out better on the other side.

16

Blindsided

KAELIN:

Not long after Karter's birth, a ministry called Israel Collective contacted us about being part of a trip to Israel they were currently putting together for influencers like us. Going to the Holy Land, to Israel, just the two of us, had the potential to be a second honeymoon. Leaving Karter was going to be very difficult, especially for Kyrah, but we needed the time away.

Kyrah and I jumped at the chance. Well, I jumped. She had to be persuaded. Leaving Karter at four months old made her very uneasy. However, we talked to both our mothers, and they agreed to split the time watching him, alternating every few days for the duration of the trip. While that didn't take away Kyrah's nervousness completely, having her mom watch Karter for at least half the time put her mind at ease. "She'll take care of him like I do," Kyrah said.

We'd also seen some positive changes in our relationship with Kyrah's mom. After the slap, Kyrah had stopped talking to her mom about our marriage. I felt better knowing that all our dirty laundry was our dirty laundry and no one else's. On top of that, over the previous few weeks

Kyrah's mom started asking us more and more questions about God and Jesus. Before, she'd never showed that much interest in the things of God, but now she did. Some of her terminology sounded a bit odd to our ears, but we both chalked it up to her being so new to it all. Kyrah bought her mom a Bible and encouraged her to start reading.

On our way to the airport, her mother brought up a conversation she'd had with one of her friends, whom Kyrah recognized. "Doesn't she claim to be a psychic?" Kyrah asked.

"Yes, but we didn't talk about anything like that," her mom said. Only later did we learn that she'd lied and had her friend do a palm reading for her. If we'd known that, we probably would not have left Karter with her, and the next chapter of our journey might have turned out very, very differently.

Dropping off Karter came with lots of tears for Kyrah, but once we got on the plane for the first leg to New York, the excitement of our trip set in. Or maybe we were happy to be someplace quiet. Planes can be loud, but they're nothing compared to a screaming baby. Once we landed in New York, we actually had a full day before our flight to Tel Aviv, which gave us some quality time with my grandma, who lives in Manhattan. We both tried to enjoy our time there, but Kyrah was torn. She loved our time together, but she missed Karter terribly. She asked, for the first of many times, "Wasn't there a way we could have brought him?" We both knew the answer to that question.

From the moment we landed in Tel Aviv, the trip exceeded all my greatest expectations. We met up with about fifteen other people, most of them friends we had made online over the years but were seeing in person for the first time. It was already dark when we got off the plane, but our day was far from over. From Tel Aviv, we drove to Tiberias, checked into our hotel, then had an authentic Mediterranean dinner. For a guy who ate fast food for most meals, I didn't quite know what to make of such healthy choices. By the end of the trip, I was loving the food and couldn't get enough of it.

I have no idea what time it was or where exactly we were when we finally went to bed. With the eleven-hour time difference, I never knew what time it was the whole time we were there. Only when we woke up the next morning did we realize we were staying right next to the Sea of Galilee. All my life, I've heard my dad talk about the Sea of Galilee in sermons, like when Jesus walked on the water and calmed the storm. The stories made it feel like a mythical place, like something out of Homer's *Odyssey*. As I looked out at the water, the stories now felt very, very real. They felt even more so when we got in a boat and sailed across it. We also stood where Jesus delivered his Sermon on the Mount on its shore and the place where he fed five thousand. Later we visited Magdala, Capernaum, and the Jordan River. In my typical Western mind-set, I tried to hurry from place to place. While visiting an ancient synagogue, I rushed to the front of our group right before I slipped on a step and slammed my shin into the stone. Our tour guide looked at me and said, "They made the steps slippery on purpose to stop people from rushing into the presence of God." After that, I ordered my steps. That's still one of my favorite lessons from the trip.

While we missed Karter, both of us were so caught up in the trip that we didn't have time to agonize over not being with him. At night we soaked up this amazing experience together with our friends. We hung out on the tops of the hotels, taking in the cool night air, drinking the most amazing wine I'd ever had, and talking about what was going on in our lives. I don't know if it was the fact that we were all in the Holy Land or if it was the wine, but we all opened up about our struggles like we'd known one another forever. Every day we were there, we felt closer and closer to this new group of friends. The conversations were transformative. Aside from a serious case of jet lag the first couple of days, the trip could not have gone better.

After several days in the region around Galilee, our bus took us down to Jerusalem. More accurately, we went *up* to Jerusalem because, once we left the Jordan Valley, it was all uphill to the literal city on a hill. My heart started beating fast when I caught my first glimpse of it up ahead of us. *How did anyone ever conquer this city?* I thought to myself as our tour guide read Bible passages about Jerusalem to us. As we got closer to the city, I looked at the goats on the sides of the green hills and I pondered how Jesus must have seen this exact same sight as he approached Jerusalem for the Passover before he was crucified. Once our bus entered the city, I thought about Jesus at every turn. I have never felt closer to Him than in the city to which He will one day return.

After another incredible day of touring and a night of sharing with our friends on a rooftop in Jerusalem, we woke up ready to see what this new day might bring. Every day had been better than the day before—and every day before had been incredible. We went to the Holocaust Museum. I do not have words to describe the depths of emotion I felt there. Then we went to lunch before our scheduled trip to the Temple Mount. At lunch, Kyrah and I were sitting across from our buddies Caleb and Macy. We were engaged in a conversation when I noticed a look on Kyrah's face that told me something was wrong. "What's up?" I asked.

KYRAH:

Before we left for our trip, my mom had talked about her desire to get into social media and maybe even write a book someday. Until that afternoon in Jerusalem, I didn't realize that she planned to use Karter to make that happen. All throughout our trip, she'd posted photos of her time with Karter, nothing too over the top, but enough for me to start feeling a little uncomfortable. After the first month of his life, Kaelin and I decided to limit how often we showed Karter and set limits as to what we revealed of his life. Obviously, with a channel called *The Edwards Family*, the entire family would be a part of our regular content. However, he was obviously too young to consent to being on camera, so in order to protect our child's long-term privacy, we preferred to keep him in the background as much as possible. We had already built the majority of our audience as "Kaelin and Kyrah" before Karter was born and even before I was pregnant, so recentering our channel around us and our relationship growth was second nature.

While sitting in the café in Jerusalem, I saw how my mom had done the opposite. And her strategy had worked. Her photos of Karter received far more attention than those without, in large part by poaching our followers who wanted to see more of Karter! She even posted a photo of Karter naked in the bathtub. I could hardly believe my eyes. I showed it to Kaelin, and he was as concerned as I was. "Okay, I have to say something," I said.

"Of course you do," Kaelin agreed.

"I hate to do it because I don't think she'll take it well, but what choice do we have?" I asked.

"None," Kaelin said. "Karter is our child. We don't know the long-term effects of oversharing. We have to be fair to him and protect his privacy."

"Agreed," I said. I then composed a short text that said, "Can you please not post photos of Karter anymore? We really want to respect his privacy," and hit send. It was early afternoon in Jerusalem, with an eleven-hour time difference with California. I didn't do the math to figure out exactly what time it was there.

My mom quickly responded with a thumbs-up emoji. I know my mom. She doesn't do thumbs-up emoji texts. A few moments later, a barrage of texts began blowing up my phone. They came while we were at lunch and when we were on the steps of the Temple Mount and as we walked the streets of the old city of Jerusalem. More texts came as we toured the Church of the Holy Sepulchre and the empty tomb and everywhere else we walked that day. I never responded, but still the texts kept coming in. My mom declared she had to keep posting photos of Karter. She spoke of our baby boy like he was somehow her reason for being alive. Something felt very, very off about what she said, and it made me worry for our child's overall well-being in her care.

There's so much more I could say about this, but out of respect for everyone's privacy, I will sum it all up by saying that this text conversation and the rest of my communication with my mom cast a dark cloud over the remainder of our dream trip to Israel. All I wanted to do was get back home and take care of my little boy myself. Going home, we were scheduled to spend another day in New York before returning to California. We canceled all of that and got home as quickly as we could.

More drama awaited us when we returned to Bakersfield. Karter was fine, but my relationship with my mother changed through the course of this interaction, and it has never been the same. When I was in high school, we were more like best friends than mother and daughter. We don't have much of a relationship today. As we documented in a couple of very long videos on our channel, much of her wrath was directed at Kaelin more so than at me. When I stood with my husband and defended him against the baseless accusations she leveled at him, I too found myself completely on the outside looking in with her. When she couldn't divide Kaelin and me into opposing teams, she separated herself from both of us. Worst of all, she did her best to make what should have been a private family matter as absolutely public as possible.

Genesis 2:24 says that when you marry, you leave father and mother and cleave to your spouse and become one flesh with them. I had trouble with the leaving part for a long time. Slowly I learned to stop leaning on my mom for my emotional support. I stopped spilling my guts about everything going on in my marriage. Through trial and error, I learned that in marriage you protect each other by working through your problems together confidentially—not by sharing them with family and friends. Now, after the storm unleashed by the simple act of asking my mother to stop sharing photos of our child on social media, I really didn't have anyone else to turn to other than my husband. In the process, I learned this is how it should have been all along. I'm not saying that you shouldn't have a good relationship with your parents after marriage. However, when you pledge your life to another, that person is your first priority, not your mom or dad or extended family. Only then can a marriage truly thrive.

KAELIN:

One day in the middle of this mess, I was about to get in the shower when my phone started buzzing on the bathroom counter. I started to ignore it, but then it kept buzzing and buzzing and buzzing. I picked it up and found messages from family and friends all over the country, messages that included screenshots of Instagram and Facebook posts from Kyrah's mom about me, posts filled with horrible lies about me. While she'd originally shared these posts with her friends, they'd quickly jumped over into the social media world where we are known.

The fallout from Kyrah's mom's posts hit quick. She received tens of thousands of views and likes, along with flaming comments that essentially told me that a large group was out there waiting for us to fall. People began unsubscribing from our channel, while more and more negative comments poured out against me. Kyrah's mom called me abusive and controlling and claimed that I had brainwashed Kyrah, and people believed her. They wanted to believe the worst about me, even when the worst was in no way true. This was my first deep dive into the downside of fame. I realized our lives as portrayed on YouTube exist for many solely for their entertainment. They didn't see us as real people, but as the actors we basically were in our old prank videos. A portion of the audience who came to watch us wanted something catastrophic to happen, something they could talk about with their friends. I do not believe this part of the audience is large, but they are vocal in the comments sections.

For me, reading the comments of those who were eager to see me fall took me right back to the dark place I was in when our channel's monetization failed. The earlier incident showed me the ugly truth that I loved money and had sacrificed too much to chase after success. And now came this. I had worked so many long hours, had been emotionally absent from my wife, all to build up a subscriber base of those I'd told myself had come along to do life with us. I'd become a workaholic, neglecting everything else, for them. And now many of them had turned against us. I hadn't realized how those who are eager to see you rise are just as eager to see you fall. Why had I ever prioritized this audience over my wife and family?

With the accusations from Kyrah's mom, I found myself in a no-win situation. If I responded and tried to refute her, I'd only feed the fire. Those who already thought the worst about me would take everything I said and twist it in a way to make me look even more guilty. But if I said nothing, my silence might be taken as a confirmation of all charges. For a few months, Kyrah and I didn't say a thing, but eventually we felt we had no choice. By then, much of the damage had been done.

However, through this we discovered the truth of Joseph's words after his brothers sold him into slavery in Egypt, what one intends for evil, God uses for good (see Genesis 50:20). Over the first year of our marriage, Kyrah and I struggled to get on the same team. After this experience, we were welded tight to each other. Kyrah had also struggled to find her voice and speak up for herself. Through this drama, she found it and she used it. When her mother tried to tear her down and post horrible things about her, Kyrah stood up to her mom. We still had lots of tears, but my wife came out of this so much stronger than before.

I also came out changed. Not only did the false accusations fired at me help put work in its proper place, but I also used them to search my heart and my life to see *WHY* some found them so easy to believe. The accusations were not true, but was there anything that might give them credence? I felt like I was on trial, and I owed it to my family, friends, and audience to be tried by fire. More importantly, I owed it to myself to look retrospectively at the type of person I had been, the things I had done, and the way I had made people feel. As I looked back over my life, there were things I was not proud of. I saw areas in which I needed to improve as a husband and a man. The first steps of change came through tough conversations with everyone around us we trusted to hold us accountable, beginning with our church family. I wasn't quite prepared for how much God planned to use them to change us as well.

KYRAH:

The drama with my mother that started when Kaelin and I were in Israel never really ended. Instead, it grew increasingly worse, and still today, my relationship with my mom is beyond strained.

As painful as that reality may be, the experience forced me to take a long look at myself and the relationships in my life. When I was a girl, I didn't feel like I knew anything about myself. I didn't assert myself but often just went along with the flow. Not anymore. My sense of self-worth does not flow from the love and praise I receive from other people, nor does love withheld wreck me as it once did. I have a confidence that flows from knowing that I am a child of God, whose love for me is truly unconditional. I've had those I love dearly turn on me and call me unspeakable things. Perhaps they hoped I'd be crushed and come crawling to them, but the only crawling I did was to the foot of the cross, to the One who had insults hurled at Him by those He called his own. Jesus told his disciples that following Him comes at a cost. In Luke 12:53, He said, "They will be divided, father against son and son against father, mother against daughter and daughter against mother." When I first read that verse, I didn't get it.

Now I do. Not only is my faith so much stronger as a result; I am stronger as well.

I am also thankful for the crisis that turned into a daily reality because it made Kaelin and me closer than ever. We learned to lean on each other for strength. On the days I struggled, Kaelin was stronger and gave me the support I needed. On the days he struggled, I gave him support. While I don't want to live through that kind of family drama again, I can honestly say it made our marriage much stronger. I am amazed at how God brought good things out of an awful situation.

17

No More Secrets

KAELIN:

After we returned from Israel, and while the fallout from our very public dispute with Kyrah's mom continued, our church small group became more important to us than ever before. Kyrah even signed up for a women's group in order to build more community and ended up meeting her now best friend Katy. I added a separate men's group to my schedule. It's funny, but the more we connected with our church groups, the closer Kyrah and I grew to each other. Although the members in our groups were all older than us, we became very close friends. My men's group consisted of teachers and doctors and other professional men. All of us leaned on one another and confided in one another. Listening to their stories about their struggles opened my eyes to my own in a freeing way.

I became especially close to Trevor, our small group leader. Even though he was older than me, our life situations weren't that different. He was also so open and honest about his own personal struggles that he encouraged me to be as well. From the beginning of my relationship with Kyrah, I'd kept part of my past hidden from her. I told myself that this past didn't matter, that I was the old Kaelin back then, the pre-Jesus-following Kaelin. However, the more time I spent with Trevor and some of the other guys in our group, the more I realized that some of our struggles were connected to the secrets I guarded so tightly. If the two of us were truly going to become one, I had to open up. Hopefully, as I did, it might help us move past some areas of marriage that had never been quite right.

After one men's group meeting, I came home and told Kyrah, "We need to talk." What followed were a series of conversations over the course of several weeks where I shared secrets with her that I'd never told anyone, secrets that went back nearly as far as I could remember. I started with when I was little, probably five or six years old. My siblings and I went over to spend the night with another family. The family was one my parents trusted, with kids and lots of their cousins around the same age as us. Basically, it was a huge slumber party with both boys and girls, but we were all relatively young, so the adults didn't think much about it.

That night, all the kids were outside, playing games and having fun, while the adults were talking. At one point, the games turned into girls smearing whipped cream on their faces and then trying to smear the whipped cream on the boys. One girl about my age chased me down to smear the whipped cream on me. I took off running and laughing, but the laughing stopped when she caught me and kissed me on the forehead. As soon as she did, I burst into tears. My siblings and the other older kids tried to calm me down. They told me I should enjoy getting kissed and not cry over it, but that only made me cry harder. Where we lived, boys didn't cry, especially not over having a girl kiss him. But I couldn't help myself. Eventually my mom was called, and she came over to take me home.

Unfortunately, that wasn't the end of the episode. I had to see all those kids at church, and when they saw me, they all teased me for freaking out. Looking back, I don't know if they actually said something or if the looks on their faces said it all. They didn't have to say much to make me feel bad around them. I knew what had happened was in the back of their minds—it was in mine, at least. I'd learned my lesson. If I ever found myself in a situation like that again, I'd go along with whatever was happening. I'd rather be traumatized than made fun of.

Eventually the teasing died down. My siblings and I spent a lot of time over at the same family's home. The place was always full of kids, and we all played games and had the kind of fun kids have. That is, until one night when one of the girls had several of her friends over. There had to be around twenty kids there that night. All the girls were in one room and the boys were in another, at least at the start. Eventually we all ended up in the same room. Someone had thrown blankets over chairs, making what I thought were forts. Pillows were also thrown around. Then the music started, and the guys and girls all paired off and began dancing. The dancing turned into grinding and kissing and I guess just getting their curiosities out on one another. My head was kind of spinning, trying to make sense of what was going on, when the girl who had kissed me a few months earlier started coming on to me. Now, I vividly remembered what had happened before, and I wasn't going to make that mistake again. The two of us sort of fell in line and started doing what everyone else was doing. When the older kids saw us, they egged us on and praised us for joining in. I was like, *Okay, I get it now.* Besides, I enjoyed doing what we were doing. It wasn't sex, but it was a lot more body contact, even though we were fully clothed, than should have been going on at our age.

The sleepovers continued and so did the fun, only now the fun and games all had a very strong sexual bent to them. Almost all the girls were older than me, yet I found age didn't matter. Everyone had a turn with these older girls, including me. While I never went all the way with any of them, my experiences went far beyond what a child should be exposed to. I found myself torn because I wanted to push the envelope, I wanted to go further, and yet I was terrified over how easily I could get these girls to do whatever I wanted. At these parties, I also witnessed older kids doing much more than I did. The experience was scarring. My perception of what constitutes a healthy expression of sexuality became warped. Love meant dominating, taking control, using people as a means to an end.

KYRAH:

"How did no one know what was going on?" was my first question when Kaelin told me about what had happened to him as a child. "You were a pastor's kid. Why weren't the parents extra protective and, you know, sticking their heads in the room every once in a while to check on you guys?"

"They did sometimes, but we were sneaking in and out," Kaelin replied. "My sister walked in on it one night and she threatened to tell on everyone. But she didn't. She didn't really know how consistently *everything* was going on. She wasn't there much. If she had been, she would have told."

"I just can't believe nothing ever leaked out," I said.

"We did get 'caught' sometimes, but I think the parents gave us the benefit of the doubt," Kaelin said. I could tell that talking about all of this made him feel very ashamed. The whole incident made me so sad for my husband. He'd been just a child. Peer pressure had led to his innocence being taken, and no one had been there to protect him. He'd been too young to even fully understand what was going on. My heart just broke.

I also couldn't help but think about how different my childhood had been. My mom and dad had never let me spend the night at anyone's house, especially if that friend had brothers. They had protected us. I wish someone had done the same for Kaelin.

KAELIN:

I felt like I didn't just need to tell Kyrah about the sleepovers. I also needed to tell her how the experiences had affected me. By the time the sleepovers had ended, the damage had been done. I went on to apply the lessons I'd learned about seduction and manipulation to all my "dating" relationships before Kyrah. I found that since I had experience with girls three or four years older than me, those my age were easier to seduce. They had no idea what they were getting themselves into when I came along. I can hardly even write about this now. I feel nothing but shame and revulsion over what I did. Although I never had intercourse, I manipulated girls into doing things they had not done before, and certainly shouldn't have done with me. I bragged about what I'd done in the locker room because being a womanizer was praised. Yet, when I was alone, I couldn't help feeling ashamed for "turning these girls out."

The tipping point came when I was a freshman in high school. I found myself in the back seat of a car with my then girlfriend. It was her sister's car, and we were about to lose our virginity in it. Right before we crossed the last line and went all the way, I hesitated. I had already witnessed the lives of teens close to me be changed forever by an unplanned pregnancy. If I kept going, that is exactly the path I was going to take, yet I knew that was not the life I wanted. I felt a great conviction within my spirit, stronger than I'd ever felt before. My relationship with God was very much up in the air during this time in my life, even to the point that I doubted whether God even existed. Yet, something stopped me that night from taking a step that might have completely changed the trajectory of my life, and that something had to be God.

Rather than follow through with the act, I stopped, apologized to my girlfriend, and put my clothes back on. Later, I ended the relationship, not because of her but because of me. I could not trust myself. I felt like I needed to get her away from me for her own protection. For the next year, I didn't date anyone. I had a lot to figure out, about myself and God and girls and my goals and dreams for my life.

KYRAH:

A few years earlier, Kaelin had told me a very brief version of the story of why he'd broken up with his ex. Back then, he told me that they'd been making out and that everything had started to get out of hand but that he'd stopped. However, I did not know how they had come to the very brink of having intercourse. "How did you stop yourself?" I asked. "When you get that close, how do you not follow through?"

"My whole future basically flashed in front of me. I just couldn't go through with it. The only explanation I have is that God stopped me," Kaelin said.

"And you stopped," I said, but I had trouble wrapping my head around what he had just told me. Honestly, I was kind of surprised.

"I just couldn't," Kaelin said. "This happened right in the middle of me questioning everything about God but then coming back around and believing. He met me right there, that night, in the back seat of the car. That night changed my life."

"Okay," I said. "I believe you." And I did.

I thought all our secrets were now out in the open. A few weeks went by and Kaelin and I talked more openly and honestly than we ever had. Fallout from the episode with my mom continued to hit us, yet it seemed all of it just made Kaelin and me that much closer. I felt like we had arrived at a really good place in our marriage.

KAELIN:

Opening up about my past felt liberating. Kyrah and I felt closer than we ever had. However, I still held on to one secret because I didn't think she'd understand. It was a part of my past, but it had also reappeared during our married life. Some days I felt like I had to say something, but I always told myself that I'd only hurt Kyrah over something that was no longer a part of my life.

One evening I met up with Trevor. The two of us started talking about addictions, and he opened up about how he had once had a horrible porn addiction that had caused a lot of problems in his marriage. As he told me this, I felt like Trevor had somehow tapped into my own secrets, like he knew something about me in the moment that I tried to pretend was far in my past. But there was no way he could know. I had to come clean with someone, and this felt like the perfect moment. "You know, Trevor," I said, then took a deep breath. "I've been there. I'm still there. I still battle with porn myself."

I know he didn't know this already, but still, Trevor did not look surprised when I told him this. "I get it," he said. "I'm glad you told me. Does Kyrah know?" he asked.

"No."

"I think you need to come clean with her," he said. He then told me how he'd gone to his wife and confessed his porn use. He hadn't held anything back. "She was totally understanding," he said. "She extended me grace that allowed me to repent and heal, and the two of us to move forward. I can't tell you what a huge difference that made in our marriage."

After hearing Trevor's story, I knew what I had to do. I had to come clean with Kyrah. Since she is a godly woman, like Brandi, I felt confident she'd extend to me the same grace Brandi had given Trevor. After all, in comparison to Trevor, my addiction wasn't much of an addiction. I'd slipped a few times and kept quiet about it. I firmly believed the only way to put it totally behind me was to tell Kyrah all about it. I figured she'd appreciate my honesty.

KYRAH:

Kaelin came home from his meeting with Trevor in a great mood. We put Karter to bed and hopped in the shower together. We were probably going to cuddle up on the couch afterward and watch a show or sit in bed and talk about life. But then, while we were in the shower, Kaelin said, "Trevor opened up about something tonight."

"Okay," I said, unsure of where he was going with this.

"He told me he used to be addicted to pornography."

"Yeah."

"He told me how God set him free from it and how he opened up to Brandi and told her everything."

"That had to be a hard conversation," I said. I wondered where he was going with this story, but I thought he was just telling me what went on in their meeting.

We got out of the shower, and Kaelin paused for a moment and said, "I have something I need to tell you."

I braced myself for what he was about to say. Standing there, completely undressed, I felt so vulnerable. I hoped this wasn't going to be something major.

"I had a problem with porn when I was younger," Kaelin said. "I actually saw it the first time when I was in elementary school, and it became a regular part of my life in high school."

"Okay," I said.

"But I've also used porn since we were married. Not often, just a few times, but enough that I felt like I needed to confess it to you."

I tried to have a neutral reaction, but I felt so blindsided and disgusted with him I didn't even want to look at him as he told me.

"Why?" I asked. Suddenly our early struggles with intimacy made sense. I'd wondered why my husband hadn't wanted to have sex with me. Now I knew the answer. All this time, I thought there had been something wrong with me. Now I knew better.

"There's no excuse. I shouldn't have done it, and I am sorry that I did."

As a woman, hearing this from my husband made me feel somehow inadequate, like I wasn't attractive enough to hold his attention. "Wasn't I enough?" I asked. All of the insecurity from the first year of our marriage came rushing back. He had denied me a lot during those times, and this felt exactly like that, but worse.

"Why didn't you tell me about this earlier?" I asked.

"You didn't ask," Kaelin said.

That answer set me off. "I have to ask you specific questions for you to be honest with me? So, what else are you hiding?" I said, not quite in a yell, but close to it.

"Nothing," Kaelin said. "You reacting like this was my greatest nightmare. Trevor told me his wife showed him grace. I thought you'd do the same."

I shook my head. "I had no reason to suspect you've been lying to me. I think I deserve the grace to have a reaction." Since the day Kaelin and I first got together, I had always put him on a pedestal, like he was different from any other guy out there, and different from me. Slowly but surely, that pedestal had become smaller and smaller. This conversation knocked him off completely.

Eventually the shock wore off, and I was able to forgive fully. Looking back, it's a good thing Kaelin finally toppled off the pedestal I had him on, because putting him up on one wasn't healthy for our relationship. He could not be real; he could not be human. More than that, when he did disappoint me—and every human being will disappoint you at some point—I was *really* disappointed because I'd expected so much more from him. Don't get me wrong. I still respect him and admire him as the man of God he continues to become. But respect and a pedestal are very different. I respect him because of how he works very hard to correct his flaws and become more like Christ. We look at people on pedestals as already "perfect," which is why it's problematic.

KAELIN:

Believe it or not, the hardest part of this story for me came a few weeks after that tough conversation. It seemed we had just fully gotten over our *lapse in communication* when Kyrah stumbled into the living room. I could tell something was off by her timid demeanor. "I have something I need to tell you," she said. I didn't know if our relationship could take any more secrets. "You're going to think I'm horrible, but you admitting to watching pornography and masturbating made me really upset…" *I know this. We've been through this…*, I thought.

She continued. "I didn't remember in the moment, but after having a conversation about those things in my women's group…" *She better not say…* "I realized I haven't been completely honest, and I've watched pornography in the past and masturbated during our marriage."

I was frozen. In the most hypocritical, ironic turn of events, Kyrah admitted to engaging in the *very things* she had come down on me for. For the entirety of our relationship, and even more after our latest uncomfortable conversation, I had believed that Kyrah was as innocent as a lamb. This was unbelievable. I already had major trust issues due to the traumatic experience with her mother; now the one person I trusted completely had lied to my face when I was at my most vulnerable. Now it was my turn to be disgusted. Then I asked all the questions she had interrogated me with weeks before.

"Why didn't you tell me about this before?"

"I didn't remember," she said, which was too convenient an excuse for me to believe.

Hmmm, I thought, *so I need to ask before she'll be honest with me.* In complete disbelief, I sat quietly as she recounted these stories. I only interrupted to add, "Is there anything else you may be *forgetting*? Speak now or forever hold your peace." Eventually, she got through every story she could remember. But, to me, it wasn't the details that mattered. More important than the whos, whats, whens, and wheres was the principle of the dishonesty. In marriage, couples are supposed to be fully known and graciously loved despite their flaws. Up until our previous conversation, I had felt partially known because I'd been intentionally hiding a secret. I'd felt I was impossible to love. That fear had been confirmed by Kyrah's reaction. Yet, in a few short weeks, we'd grown past that situation and stronger because of it. We hadn't expected another test so soon, but Kyrah's secret and the irony of it was too much. I immediately jumped right back to pettiness and keeping score. *Why?* I asked myself. We had seen where score-keeping had gotten us and had both agreed not to visit that place again.

Our conversation continued for a while, and although I'd love to say I responded to Kyrah in the way I'd wanted her to respond to me, I didn't because I now felt what she'd been feeling when I'd come clean to her. Her being shocked and hurt and upset all at the same time now made sense. *How could I expect her not to feel those emotions?*

I felt my own hypocrisy as I failed to extend the grace I'd expected from her. I had the same reaction she'd had, but worse. Although I was chastised for my sin, I mocked her for hers. Neither of these approaches resembles the grace God extends to us. When I consider how a perfect, blameless Savior died in place of deceitful sinners like Kyrah and me, we couldn't point fingers at each other. We had to forgive as we have been forgiven.

KAELIN AND KYRAH:

Sharing our struggles with pornography with each other helped us learn that if you're wrong, admit it. Save yourself the time and energy of trying to deny it and take responsibility for your actions. Keeping score won't bring you together. It will drive you apart. Keeping track of wrongs suffered causes you to raise yourself above the other as if you can do no wrong. You can do wrong, and you have, probably more recently than you want to admit. Having honest conversations where you come clean are uncomfortable because you have to trust that your spouse will forgive and be willing to move on. Yet, within these difficult conversations, we learn to communicate in a healthy way and thus grow together. Trust us, we were reluctant to even share these stories in this book, but we now understand that sin grows best in the dark and the battle for a love that lasts starts in the safety of gracious communication. Therefore, have the conversations. Get the closure. Share your secrets. And open yourself up to be fully loved. But, if someone opens up to you, be careful not to make the same mistake we did, because you never know when you might need the same grace someone needs from you.

18

One Last Test to Fail

KYRAH:

A new year came, and the fallout from our family drama finally started to die down. Even better, after our trip to Israel we were able to put Karter on a more regimented sleep schedule. We set a bedtime for him every night, and he finally started going to sleep without screaming. By the time he was around six months old, he was even sleeping through the night. Kaelin and I actually had peace at night, which made us look at each other and say, "Hey, let's have another baby!" I know that sounds a little crazy, but we wanted to have our kids close together. Kaelin and his brother Kameron are only two years apart; I've always admired their relationship and hoped to have a second boy so they could experience the same bond. Kaelin is also always sharing memories with Kameron from his childhood with me, and I know how special it is to him that he has a brother close in age.

In February 2019, we decided the time was right to start trying to get pregnant. This time, unlike the first, I was prepared. I knew what we were getting ourselves into, and I was going to be ready. Rather than wait for the first signs of morning sickness to let me know I was pregnant, I bought a bunch of inexpensive pregnancy tests on Amazon. I tested myself all the time because I wanted to know if I was pregnant as quickly as possible.

On March 10, I was sitting on the couch watching television, while Kaelin was lying on his stomach on the floor with his laptop in front of him. "I need to go to the bathroom," I said as I got up to leave the room. What I didn't tell him was that I was waiting for this moment so that I could take another pregnancy test.

"Okay," Kaelin said with a tone that was basically like, *I don't know why you just told me this, but okay.*

I went down the hall and peed on the stick just like I had done several times over the past few weeks, then waited a few moments for the test to do its trick. Very slowly a word began to appear: *Pregnant.*

I didn't even pause long enough to pull my pants back up. Instead, I ran down the hall with the test in my hand. "Kaelin, I'm pregnant!"

"What! Are you serious?!" he said, jumping up from the floor. Then he stopped and looked at me with a puzzled look. "Wait, I didn't even know you were taking a test."

"Surprise!" I said.

We waited a few weeks before we told all our friends and family. When we did tell them, I always added, "Please pray for me that I won't have as much morning sickness as last time, and please pray for my labor and delivery that it will be easier than with Karter." Karter's delivery had left me so exhausted that I could hardly enjoy my first few moments with him. I prayed I could fully experience our new baby's birth.

KAELIN:

Thankfully, Kyrah did not have the same debilitating morning sickness the second time around. While she still had her moments, overall she was able to function, which she hadn't been able to do with Karter.

A couple of months went by. All the doctor visits went great. It looked like this was going to be a pretty easy pregnancy for Kyrah. But then one day she became extremely ill. She was pale and unable to sleep or eat anything. I knew this had gone far past morning sickness. She also had terrible pain in her upper abdomen and back that refused to go away. She went to her doctor, who told us, "It's probably your gallbladder. Sometimes women will have a flare-up during pregnancy. We really don't want to have to do surgery because of the risk to the baby. The best thing we can do is try to manage it until after the baby is born and reevaluate." He then sent her home with a prescription and told her to take over-the-counter pain relievers for her discomfort.

But the prescription didn't stop her symptoms, and over-the-counter pain relievers didn't put a dent in her pain, especially not on the bad days. She reached a point where she could not even get out of bed. Then a really bad day hit. Kyrah called to me from the bathroom. I could tell from her tone of voice that something was very wrong. "I just went to the bathroom and my pee…It looks like black tea," she said, very scared.

I was scared with her. "Let me help you get back into the bed so you can lie down," I said.

"Okay," she said. "I've never hurt like this in my life." I tried to figure out something to do to help her, but she insisted on taking her prescription and trying to sleep it off.

A few hours later, she came walking into the living room, where Karter and I were hanging out. "Kaelin…I'm really sick. I'm scared this might be something bad."

"I'm on it," I said. "I'll find someone who will help us." Her doctor had been very conservative thus far but that clearly was not enough. I started making calls to area hospitals and different doctors, trying to find someone who would operate on a pregnant woman. I literally would not take no for an answer.

One hospital told me to bring her in for more testing as soon as possible, so I rushed her to the emergency room, where they ran tests and determined that her gall bladder had filled with stones and some had gotten stuck in the bile duct, causing her liver to fail. They needed to take out the gallbladder. However, since she was pregnant, the surgery called for a level of expertise not available in Bakersfield. Thankfully, a hospital in Fresno, one hundred miles north, could do it. We had Kyrah transferred there first thing the next morning by ambulance. I went home to pack her a hospital bag, and Karter and I hit the road the next morning. We arrived shortly after the ambulance and Kyrah's dad.

I tried to go up to her room, but the hospital staff stopped me. "Children are not allowed to visit the hospital rooms during flu season." I tried to explain that my wife had just arrived by ambulance and she needed me, but rules were rules. "I'm sorry, but there are no exceptions," I was told.

I now faced a dilemma. I needed to be with Kyrah, but I also had to take care of our son. And I had to be the one to take care of him because I didn't trust anyone else to do it. All the drama with Kyrah's mom had given me serious second thoughts about leaving Karter with anyone, even my mom or one of my siblings. I was afraid they'd disappoint me like Kyrah's mom had. But I had to make a choice: my wife or my son. I don't like choices like that, so I came up with another option. The first day, I left Karter with Kyrah's dad for a few hours so I could see Kyrah. Every day after that, I reluctantly took Karter over to my brother's house; then I drove the two hours to the hospital in Fresno. I stayed with Kyrah all day. I then drove two hours back to Bakersfield in time to pick up Karter just before midnight. I did this every day until Kyrah's surgery.

Now keep in mind that we did not know how Kyrah's surgery was going to go, when it would happen, or if our baby she was carrying could survive it if she had it. The hospital made sure to remind us often how the surgery put him at serious risk.

Yet, as sick as Kyrah was and as dangerous as her illness was for our unborn child, I knew they were being cared for by the hospital staff. Kyrah's dad also came up to Fresno and stayed with her whenever I was gone, which meant she was never really alone. And I had to leave to go take care of Karter. I felt I had no choice.

I was wrong.

I was still traveling back and forth between Bakersfield and Fresno, juggling caring for Karter and being with Kyrah, when her doctor told us her surgery was going to be on the next day. However, he could not tell us the exact time of the surgery. When I left that evening to go pick up Karter and take him home, Kyrah said to me, "Get here early tomorrow. We don't know when they're going to take me to the OR and it could be in the morning. I need you here before I go in. Please, get here early."

I kissed her and said, "Of course. I'll get here as early as possible. I'll see you before you go into surgery and I'll be here waiting for you when you get out."

The next morning, I got up while it was still dark, rushed through our morning routine, and loaded everything up to take Karter to my brother's house. I meant to be at my brother's house for only a minute or two, but we got to talking, and before I knew it, I'd lost all track of time. I happened to glance down at my watch and said, "Oh no. I should have been at the hospital already." I ran out to the car and sped the whole way there, praying I didn't get pulled over. When I reached the hospital, I ran into the waiting area and started toward Kyrah's room. Then I saw her dad walking out, clearly shaken up.

I was too late.

I had missed seeing Kyrah before her surgery by two minutes. Literally two minutes.

KYRAH:

On the day of my surgery, I kept looking at the clock, wondering where Kaelin was. Between my intense pain and the medication, I never really knew where I was or what exactly was going on. I'd been wheeled around everywhere since I'd arrived, going from one test to the next, lying under various machines for a half hour or an hour at a time. In the beginning, I was alone until my dad came up. He checked into a hotel near the hospital so that he was always close by, even when I was asleep. Kaelin could have been there too, but he refused to leave Karter with anyone. I knew that he was having a hard time trusting anyone, but I felt that my condition should have taken precedent. I wasn't just sick. The doctors told me that if I had the surgery, we could lose the baby or the baby could suffer severe defects that we couldn't detect until birth. If I didn't have the surgery, both the baby and I might not make it. The best-case scenario for not having the surgery was spending the rest of this pregnancy in the hospital, which still left me at high risk of losing the baby or losing my own life or both.

After the doctor told us that, I looked at Kaelin and said, "I am your wife. I need you here. Karter will be fine with your mom. I am not fine. I shouldn't have to make any of these decisions by myself." Kaelin said he could take care of both me and the baby, but he couldn't.

I was just thankful my dad was there. His being there meant so much to me. After the fallout with my mom, I'd felt like I didn't have any immediate family left. My younger brother and sisters felt torn, and they naturally sided with our mom. They mainly heard her side because when you're a kid, you expect your parents to tell you the whole truth. I didn't blame them for siding with her, but I missed them.

I called my dad one day shortly after the fallout with my mom and asked if we could grab lunch and talk. By now he and my mom had separated. My dad and I then had one of the most honest conversations I'd ever had with him. Our relationship improved so much afterward. Since

I'd started high school, my mom had continually told me so many horrible things about my father, and I always believed her because, like I wrote before, she was my mom. Of course I believed her. But believing my mom caused a lot of damage to my relationship with my dad. I knew my parents had a lot of problems, but my mom, in her own effort to save her marriage, told us we needed to always forgive my dad even though he was awful. I know, it doesn't make a lot of sense to me as I write it, but that's what happened. Even though my mom had been so miserable in her marriage, she was scared of losing the life she'd spent most of her life building. Yet, at the same time, she told me that my dad was a horrible person who couldn't be trusted.

Now that I was on the outs with my mom, I saw all she'd told me about my dad in the past in a different light. He's not perfect. He'll be the first to tell you that. I don't expect him to be, but I wanted him to own up to his own past mistakes and try to do better. It would've been easy for him to blame my mom for everything now that they had separated, but he chose to focus on fixing the problems of his own making, and that speaks a lot to his character and who he was becoming. My dad hadn't always been around, but I was incredibly thankful to have him around in a more meaningful way now.

I don't know where I would have been without my dad on the day of my surgery. Like I said, I kept watching the clock, wondering where Kaelin was. He told me he'd be there early. "If he doesn't get here on time, I will be so mad," I told my dad. My dad said something to try to calm me.

More time passed, and Kaelin still wasn't there. Finally, the nurse came in and said, "We're ready to take you back now."

I looked at my dad, afraid that if I spoke, I'd burst into tears. "Don't worry, Kyrah," he said as he held my hand. "I'll stay with you as long as they'll let me." When the orderlies came and started wheeling me out, my dad walked beside me, talking with me, telling me not to worry, that everything was going to be okay. I tried to believe him, and I really wanted to, but I was so scared for the baby, and I was so mad at Kaelin for not being there. But being mad wasn't going to do me any good right then, so I told myself, *He's not here. There's nothing I can do about it now.*

They took me directly to the pre-op area, where they prepared me for surgery. My anxiety level shot up, and I could feel my heart pounding through my body. I started sweating even though I was freezing. My mouth felt heavy and watery, like I was about to vomit. The room was spinning, but I was trying to keep composed. I knew I needed to make it to the bathroom before I threw up in front of everyone. Gathering all my strength, I calmly walked the long hallway to the bathroom, trying not to be conspicuous. The moment I was around the corner and out of sight I ran the rest of the way. "Oh, God," I prayed, "I am so scared. I need Your peace. Please give me Your peace."

By the time I walked out of the bathroom and back to the gurney, my heart rate had settled down and a sense of peace covered me. My fear for myself and for my baby disappeared. I knew that whatever happened, God had this.

The nurse asked me if I was okay. I smiled and told him I was. He reconnected the IV. I was trying to look around at where I was and what my doctors looked like. Then everything happened so quickly, and I'm glad it did. They inserted a new IV and, without warning, started placing a mask over my nose and mouth and asking me to take three deep breaths. I thought they were just giving me oxygen, but that's the last thing I remember before waking up.

KAELIN:

Kyrah's dad could barely look at me. He didn't have to say anything. I already felt bad enough for not being there before she went into surgery. He and I made our way up to the OR waiting area, found a seat, and stared at the monitor that showed where they were in Kyrah's surgery. The tension was tangible as we sat, silently gazing at the screen. I could tell he had words for me and was waiting for the opportunity to let me have them. I didn't know how he would react. I could only imagine what a father might say to a son-in-law who had effectively just abandoned his daughter at the most vulnerable time in her life. I know what I would say. I also know what Kyrah's mom would have said. We'd had our exchanges. But I'd never had any confrontations with Kyrah's dad. He's a much more calculating personality. When he speaks, there's an intentionality not only in his words, but also in the timing.

So, we sat there in silence. Looking back, I now understand he wanted the consequences of my decisions to completely sink in. His silence was an interrogation. All he had to do was look at me and I knew how deeply I'd disappointed him. He saw how hurt Kyrah was when I was not there for her.

His silence kept screaming at me. Finally, I couldn't take it anymore. "The surgery should only last a little while longer."

Why would I lead with that? He doesn't care how long the surgery is. He cares about the well-being of his daughter. Thankfully he didn't hear me. I tried to take a more appropriate stab at it. "Her surgeon told us yesterday that he's confident the procedure would be a success and that the baby would be exposed to as little radiation as possible," I said.

Her dad gave me a nod and seemed comforted with the information. More awkward silence followed—awkward for me, not him. Over the next couple of hours, we talked a little, but we never quite got to the conversation we needed to have. Then, when I thought I might get off the hook, he opened up and started talking about his own struggles in marriage. Basically, he told me what he wished he would've done, going back to the very beginning of his marriage. He'd made mistakes. He didn't want to see me do the same. That's why it hurt so much for him to see me falling into the same trap he did of putting his work and even his children before his relationship with his wife. He also saw himself in me as I hurt my wife the way he did his. "It's too late for me," he told me, "but not for you. Your wife has to come first. Before Karter. Before work. Especially before you."

I don't know if I've ever had a more transformational conversation in my life. He wasn't trying to fix me. Instead, he related to me through his experience. He told me where his choices had taken him, and it was a place neither one of us wanted to see me end up.

After that talk, I made arrangements with my mom and brother to take care of Karter, both day and night, until Kyrah got out of the hospital. Then I got a room at the same hotel where Kyrah's dad had been staying. Aside from short trips to the hotel to take a shower and sleep, I stayed at Kyrah's side throughout her remaining ten-day hospital stay. I tried to get the staff to let me sleep in the chair in Kyrah's room, but they kicked me out late at night. I was always back before she woke up the next day. I'd failed this test once. I didn't want to fail again. A lot of parents make the mistake of putting their children over their relationship with their spouse. They end up being nothing more than parenting partners, rather than lovers. I love Kyrah. Ephesians 5:25 says that husbands are to love their wives like Christ loves the church. I hadn't been very good at doing that in the past. I was determined to do better in the future.

KYRAH:

After the surgery, I could still barely open my eyes, but I had to know. "Is my baby okay?" I asked the nurse.

"The baby is fine. You both came through the surgery without any problems."

Thank you, Jesus, I prayed. Then I said, "My husband better be here."

"We'll be taking you back to your room soon," she said. "You can have visitors there and we'll call him for you."

When I finally did get back to the room, I didn't see anyone. A few minutes later, he walked in. I don't remember what I first said to him since I was still kind of out of it, but I'm pretty sure I let him know how unhappy I was with him not being here for me before they wheeled me into surgery. Kaelin joked, "Don't you remember? I was here the whole time."

I shot him a look that let him know I didn't think he was very funny at all.

"I'm sorry, Kyrah," he said. "I should have been here. There's no excuse. I should have been here."

Kaelin didn't just say the words. Over the next week and a half, while I recovered in the hospital, he never left my side until the nurses kicked him out at night. Then he was back first thing in the morning. When I finally got to go home, he became far more attentive to my needs. During my recovery, he helped me shower and he took care of Karter and he brought me whatever I told him I needed. Before, there had been times when I'd felt like work was more important to Kaelin than I was. After I got home from the hospital, it was like I could feel his love for me. I could tell he wanted to be thoughtful and use his actions to show his love for me, even when it didn't benefit him in any way. This was all I ever felt like I was missing from him.

KAELIN:

A couple of months after Kyrah recovered from her surgery, my best friend, Brandon, called me up one day. Brandon and I have been friends since we met on the football field all the way back in second grade. He was the quarterback and I was the running back. Though we were inseparable for most of our lives, after junior high, we never went to the same school again. I was sure we would stop being friends with how little we talked, but similar to Kyrah and Daja, time and distance had virtually no effect on our friendship. For us, it helps that we're very alike and share the same interests. In elementary school it was our obsession with football. In junior high it was video games, and then in high school it was girls, and subsequently it was our faith rebirth. We are so close because it seems like we are literally going through the same seasons of life at the same time, no matter how often we speak or hang out. From breakups to tough school decisions, we've always had each other to talk things through.

At the time, our latest shared experience was young marriage. He had recently gotten married to his high school sweetheart, Jessica, about a year after Kyrah and I got married. After they got married, they moved to El Paso, Texas, where Brandon had just gotten a football scholarship to play quarterback. Judging by the date and time of the call, I knew Kyrah and I might be getting an invitation to come out to Texas to see him play. I was correct.

After catching up on FaceTime for about twenty minutes, I got the news I was expecting. "Our schedule just came out," he said, "and we have a HUGE game against Texas Tech in Lubbock this fall. You and Kyrah should come out and watch it." We'd driven over to Vegas to watch him play against the University of Nevada, Las Vegas, the season before. And through the years we had gone to a few of his high school and junior college games as well. It was a little tradition between Brandon and Jessica and Kyrah and me. We did a bunch of things together, but traveling and watching games together was one of our favorites.

"Bro, you already know I'm down," I said. "We'll have to check with Kyrah's doctors to make sure she can still travel then, being pregnant and all."

"It's one of the first games of the year, so hopefully she can travel. It will be good to see you guys. Besides, you've talked forever about maybe moving to Texas someday. This will give you a chance to see what you're missing out on," Brandon said.

He was right. Even after we'd dropped our crazy plan to elope and move to Austin, I'd never turned loose of the idea of moving to Texas someday. Something about it captivated my imagination. Maybe it was the lower cost of living and the fact that Texas doesn't have an income tax. That definitely appealed to me. I also liked the idea of raising a family in a place less socially volatile than California. Bakersfield is a pretty conservative area, but you never know what kinds of laws the state of California might pass. Or maybe my desire to move went back to my longing to break away from the Bakersfield mind-set. Don't get me wrong. Kyrah and I had a good life there, but I couldn't shake the feeling that life might be better somewhere else, maybe somewhere like the Lone Star State.

"I'll let you know," I told Brandon. After getting the green light from Kyrah's doctors, I called Brandon back and told him we were in. I couldn't wait.

KYRAH:

When Kaelin asked about flying out to Texas for a couple of weeks, I was all for it. We'd talked so much about Texas that I really wanted to see it. Karter was now old enough to travel with us without us feeling like we had to rent a truck to haul all his baby equipment with us. I was also still far enough from my due date with the second baby that I could still fly without worrying about giving birth at thirty thousand feet. The timing felt perfect, so I told Kaelin, "Let's go for it."

We didn't just go for Brandon's football game. Kaelin and I spent two weeks in Texas. We drove down to Lubbock for the game, but we also spent a lot of time in Dallas and Austin. The trip was supposed to be a vacation, but since we had come so close to moving there a couple of years earlier, it soon turned into a "What did we miss out on?" trip. Then it evolved into a "Could we really consider living here?" trip. By the time we got on the plane to fly back to Bakersfield, it started to become a "Do we really want to get on the plane and leave here?" trip. Frankly, I loved it there. I loved

Dallas and I loved Austin and I loved the people and I loved the food and the scenery and everything about the place. Honestly, I was surprised. I told Kaelin, "You know, I can actually see us living here."

"So why don't we stay and have our stuff shipped out here?" he replied, half-serious.

I was tempted. However, the memory of my difficult delivery with Karter was very fresh in my mind. I was less than three months from my due date. I did not want to have to find a new ob-gyn so late in my pregnancy. I also remembered how we'd made so many major changes in our lives right before Karter was born. We'd had a new house built and moved in just a couple of weeks before he was born. All the changes in life had made my postpartum adjustment that much harder. This time around, I wanted to minimize stress and focus on giving our new baby the best possible start in life. "Maybe like a year after the baby is born I'll be ready to discuss it," I said.

"That's fine," Kaelin said. "It's not like we have to move or anything like that. It would be fun to move someplace new and have a whole new start together, but we have time. There's no rush. We have our whole lives in front of us."

I smiled. I loved the sound of that. We did have our whole lives together, and I felt like we were now more connected than we'd ever been. Whether we stayed in Bakersfield for the rest of our lives or moved to the other side of the country or the world, whatever we faced, we faced together. We'd already been through a couple of really hard tests, and they'd only made our relationship stronger. I felt confident that no matter what the future held, we'd be okay.

19

New Beginning

KYRAH:

I woke up around midnight to the feeling of something trickling down my leg. *What the heck?* I said to myself as I struggled to wake up enough to grasp what had just happened. When I flopped into bed two hours before, I'd fallen asleep so fast that I didn't even remember my head hitting the pillow. The day before had not been especially exhausting, but at nine months pregnant, I was always tired.

Now I sat up in the bed, disoriented. I felt the leg of my shorts. They were soaked. *I can't believe I just peed the bed. What am I, two?* I stumbled into the bathroom, trying not to wake Kaelin. My mind had not caught up with my body because, once in the bathroom, I sat there for several minutes, trying to decide if I needed to change the sheets or just my shorts. *But my legs are wet too.* I grabbed a towel to dry myself when it hit me: My water had just broken. Now my mind started racing. I needed to take a quick shower and change my clothes and wake Kaelin and call my dad to come stay with Karter and get to the hospital as quickly as possible because this baby could come at any second and I needed to do it all right now because hard contractions would hit at any moment. Didn't hard contractions always come as soon as your water broke? That's what I'd always heard.

"Kaelin," I said as I walked back into the bedroom. "Wake up. My water just broke."

"Are you sure?" he mumbled, still half-asleep.

"Yeah, I'm sure. We have to get to the hospital immediately."

"Can you wait?" he asked.

"Uhh, no…We have to get ready now."

I hopped into the shower, and Kaelin joined me a few minutes later. I kept waiting for the first hard contraction, but it never came. Instead, I had the same kind of contractions I'd felt when I first went into labor with Karter.

Once I was dressed, I called my dad and told him what was going on. My dad and Karter were buddies now. I knew Karter would be in good hands while we brought his brother into the world. When I hung up the phone with my dad, I looked around the house. It was a mess. Even though today was my original due date for the baby, I hadn't done much to have the house ready for guests to come over. I walked around, picking up Karter's toys and shoving dishes into the dishwasher. The last thing I wanted was for my dad to have to stay in a messy house.

By the time my father arrived, my contractions were five minutes apart and painful. "We need to go," I told Kaelin. I knew from Karter's birth that really hard labor was just around the corner. If I'd timed everything right, I was going to be just about ready for an epidural by the time I got checked into the hospital. I was in labor with Karter for twenty-eight hours. Since my water had already broken, I didn't think this labor would last as long, but I prepared myself for the worst. Even if this baby came faster, I'd had to push four full hours with Karter, and even then, they'd had to use a vacuum for the delivery. I was prepared for this to go on for quite a while.

The sun still had not come up by the time I settled into my labor and delivery room in the hospital. I prepared myself for a long stay. With Karter, I'd had no idea what to expect, either through the labor process or after he was born. Now I did. I was ready for whatever labor and delivery experience life was going to throw at me, but I prayed for a peaceful one. Kaelin and I had also stockpiled several weeks' worth of YouTube posts to give both of us some time off work after the baby arrived. We'd had such a hard time after the first birth and had learned from those mistakes.

My labor pains continued. I slept between them the best I could until they became uncomfortable enough that I needed an epidural so that I could rest. By now we were only six hours into my labor. I knew I needed to get as much rest as I could now, before everything became crazy. Kaelin grabbed some sleep in a recliner in the room. Around eight or nine, Kaelin left to make sure Karter got to day care on time. When he returned, his mother was with him. She was so excited to meet her new grandson. "I think I still have a long way to go," I told her.

Except I didn't.

At noon, the nurse assured me that the baby would be here in the next few hours. Moments later, I felt movement and shifting in my belly and thought to myself, *What an interesting feeling*. A few minutes later, my regular OB doctor came in to check on me for the first time that morning. He told me I was dilated to nine centimeters, but when I contracted, I was at ten centimeters. He had me do a practice push at the next contraction. I gasped and told him, "I think the baby is coming out!!" Feeling my body birth my baby made me so happy I couldn't stop smiling. I was nervous I wouldn't be able to feel anything, like my delivery with Karter, because of the epidural. I felt an enormous amount of excitement and couldn't wait to get going.

He immediately told me to stop pushing and said, "You're right, the baby is coming." In seconds, the entire room was flipped around, nurses came piling in, and my bed was being reclined. We jumped from settling in for a long labor to high alert. "Okay, next contraction I want you to push hard," the doctor said. I did as I was told. I pushed and pushed and as I did, I felt my baby coming down the birth canal. It sort of freaked me out because I hadn't experienced any of that with Karter.

"Okay, keep pushing with every contraction," the doctor said with an urgent tone of voice.

The baby's head was out, but his shoulders were stuck for a few moments. I could tell the doctors were running through different scenarios for getting him the rest of the way out. They settled on another fourth-degree episiotomy, and after just ten minutes of pushing, my second baby boy was born.

I looked up at Kaelin, who had huge tears in his eyes. "You did it," he said. "I am so proud of you."

"Thank God, thank God, thank God," I said. He had answered my prayers and given me the peaceful delivery experience I'd hoped for. I was alert and able to take everything in. At this point, Kaelin and I didn't know if we'd have another baby. I was so thankful that I was able to be fully present for his birth. We also did not have to live through another round of the NICU.

We named our baby Kaiser. In the remaining months of pregnancy, we had narrowed our baby names down to Konnor and Kaiser. Ultimately, we felt the name Konnor just didn't feel right and settled on Kaiser because it was unique and we felt like it fit our family.

Once we brought Kaiser home, I noticed another huge answer to prayer. I did not go into the depths of postpartum depression I'd experienced before. Within a couple of weeks, I started to feel like myself again. Obviously, my body had a huge transition to make, but mentally and emotionally I felt a thousand times better than during our first experience with a new baby in the house. I'd prepared myself for the worst, but thankfully, we were pleasantly surprised.

I also had a much easier time with Kaiser after we brought him home from the hospital than I'd had with Karter. It's not that Kaiser was necessarily an easier baby. I think it really had more to do with the fact that I knew what to expect. The first few days were baby heaven for both boys, but when I had the sudden emotional plunge on the third day of Kaiser's life, I didn't panic like I had before. I knew my hormones were settling and that it was just a transition. Kaiser cried in the middle of the night, like all babies do, but I expected it this time around. We put Kaiser on a regular sleeping schedule much sooner than we did Karter, which also helped a lot. I still had days of bursting into tears, but I knew why I was crying. I felt the weight of the responsibility of another child, but I also knew this was a normal emotion to go through. One of my friends from our small group, Katy, visited me in the hospital and brought me a gift basket with treats and fuzzy blankets and socks. She assured me that she was going to set up all the women in our group on a food rotation to bring meals the first couple weeks of Kaiser's life. My friends not only brought meals; they also cleaned and held the baby and did other things to help us through those first few weeks. In a word, they were incredible.

KAELIN:

Kaiser was born on December 13. Just over two weeks later, New Year's Eve rolled around. Now, New Year's Eve is a pretty special day to both Kyrah and me because that's the day I asked her to marry me. The timing felt perfect with the New Year giving us a new start to our relationship. Those first couple of years had had their ups and downs, but for the past year Kyrah and I had been thriving and on the same page. The life we wanted when we had our intentions talk back in 2013 was now the life we were living. On top of that, we now had our second son. We'd talked about stopping at two children, so, in a way, our little family felt complete, like this initial phase of our married life had come to a close. I couldn't help but then think, *What's next?*

The question felt bigger than wondering where we needed to go and what we needed to do in this next phase of our life as a family. This wasn't just any new year that was about to start. January 1, 2020, marked the beginning of a whole new decade, not just on the calendar, but for Kyrah and me as well. Ten years had now passed since our little junior high romance that kicked off our life together. I kept thinking back on what had happened in those ten years. Both Kyrah and I had become completely different people. We'd gone through so many transitions, physically and spiritually and emotionally and relationally. *What could the next ten years hold for us?* I wondered.

To no one's surprise, I took out my idea notebook and I put down in words the stirring I felt in my soul. I wrote down:

Don't settle.
Strive for the best.
Make a move.
Get outside your comfort zone.
Take calculated risks.
Risk and bet on yourself.

The more I prayed and thought through these ideas running through my head, the more I felt in the core of my being that we needed to make a big change. More to the point, a big move. Kyrah and I had never really stopped talking about maybe moving someday after we almost eloped to Texas several years earlier. During our two-week trip to Texas earlier in the fall, both of us were nearly ready to find a place and have our stuff shipped out to us without even going back to Bakersfield first. If Kyrah had not been six months pregnant, we might have done it—that's how much we both loved Austin and Dallas. And now that Kaiser had been born, I didn't want us to drop the idea and move on and never revisit it. I kept thinking not only about moving, but also about why I wanted to leave the only place we'd ever known and move out of a paid-off house and go to a place halfway across the country where we'd only spent a grand total of two weeks and knew absolutely no one. Moving didn't make any sense. But then I started thinking about where we wanted to raise our boys, and I kept finding myself drawn to Texas.

We weren't the only ones wrestling with these kinds of questions. A lot of our closest friends were also going through a time of transition. Brandon and his wife, Jessica, had just moved back to Bakersfield after he'd played college football for four years. However, they didn't plan to stay. He planned on entering the NFL or CFL draft, which meant they could move away again before summer. Another close friend, Stavros, had also recently moved back after spending four years playing college football in Vancouver and was also entering the CFL draft, which meant Stavros and his wife, Kylie, were going to move away as well. With so many of our friends making major life changes, it felt like it could be our time as well. I had also grown uncomfortable being so comfortable in life. I was ready for the next challenge and the next big adventure. The only question was the timing.

About six weeks after Kaiser was born, Kyrah and I put the boys down for bed and had some time just for the two of us. "I've been thinking," I said.

Kyrah laughed. "Oh no. What about this time?"

"Moving."

"To Texas?"

"Yes," I said.

"You know," Kyrah said, "I've been thinking about that too, and you know what, I think we should do it."

I nearly fell off the couch. "Are you serious?" I asked.

"Yeah. I mean, I really liked Austin and Dallas, and I can see myself living in either place. I thought we'd probably have to wait a long time, but Kaiser is doing great and I feel so much better this time than last time. Why not? I think a fresh start is a great idea. Besides, the one thing that always tied me to Bakersfield was my family. I felt guilty about moving away from them, but with everything that's happened, I don't know that it wouldn't be good for us to have some distance between us and our families."

"Wow. I was not expecting that answer. If you're actually ready to move, I can get everything sorted out," I said.

"I am," Kyrah said.

I dove into researching the Dallas metropolitan area. We chose Dallas over Austin because, even though we loved both places, Dallas is a major city with everything we could ever want to experience, from shopping to sports to recreation. The airport also offered nonstop service to nearly every place we'd ever want to go, including our hometown of Bakersfield. Thanks to the DFW Airport, we could get back to our families in three hours if something came up.

As for finding an apartment, I knew we wanted a modern, three-bedroom apartment with lots of natural light. Even though Karter was still a few years away from starting school, I researched the best school districts in the area. From my experience, I'd learned that good schools equaled a good place to live. Eventually my search led me to Frisco, an up-and-coming city just outside of Dallas. We'd only driven through during our visit, but all signs pointed toward it being the place to live. I then went apartment shopping online and found one that looked like a perfect fit. After filling out an online application and making a few phone calls, we had our place. I didn't exactly have the keys in hand, but they were waiting for us at the apartment office.

KYRAH:

Kaelin ordered a moving truck, then booked plane tickets for the four of us not long after he found an apartment. When he told me we were good to go, I looked around our house and said, "There's no way we're going to be ready in time."

"We'll make it," Kaelin assured me. I wasn't so sure. For some crazy reason, we hadn't booked our flights for a couple of months out. We were set to get on a plane and move to Frisco in just a few weeks.

"How are we going to get all this done?" I asked. I was still excited about moving, but I started to wonder if we were nuts for trying to pull off a move so quickly. But, aside from our first year of dating, Kaelin and I have never really taken anything slow. We planned our wedding in a day and we were pregnant with our first child six months after that. Now we had two children under the age of two. I guess once we make up our minds, we act. We also didn't give our families a lot of time to get used to the idea of us moving. Both of us broke the news to them two weeks before we got on the plane for Dallas. To our relief, everyone seemed excited for us. No one seemed very surprised since we'd talked about making a move like this for such a long time. Of course, it might have been that no one really believed we'd go through with the move.

The two weeks flew by. When the day came to load all our stuff in the twenty-seven-foot trailer that was delivered to our home, I woke up burning up with a fever and throwing up. What perfect timing for the flu! I couldn't do much of anything but lie on the couch. Thankfully we had our friends come over and help us. The wives, Jessica and Kylie, helped me load the boxes. Then Kaelin, Brandon, and Stavros took care of the heavy stuff. Even so, loading everything took much longer than we expected. The last item went on the truck as the sun went down. We tried to sleep that night on air mattresses, but I don't know if we ever really did fall asleep.

Every time my eyes closed, I immediately started dreaming about getting on the plane the next day and flying to our new home that we'd never seen.

Very early the next morning, the alarm went off. I rolled over and looked at Kaelin. "This is it," I said. "I guess we're really moving."

"This is it," Kaelin said, and then let out a sigh. "I hope this is everything we hope it's going to be."

20

Role Reversal

KAELIN:

Our Uber pulled into our new apartment complex in Frisco just as our cars were being delivered. I smiled and said to Kyrah, "This feels like a little divine confirmation that we were supposed to make this move." It wasn't just that we'd have a way to drive. We'd also loaded down the cars with the essentials we'd need until our furniture and boxes arrived in a couple of weeks.

"It sure seems that way," Kyrah said. This move was a huge risk for both of us. For the first time in our lives, we were *completely* on our own. We didn't have anyone else to lean on for babysitting or in case of emergencies. We'd left father and mother, not just metaphorically but physically. Bakersfield was fifteen hundred miles in our rearview mirror. This was our new start in a new state in a new decade, our first decade of our fully adult life. Everything felt like it was falling into place for us.

We went to the front office to get the keys to our apartment only to discover they'd given us a unit on the second level. The complex did not have an elevator. The thought of carrying two carloads of boxes while juggling two kids under two after my friends and I had just packed a full house into a trailer didn't exactly excite me. *Oh well, it is what it is*, I thought. *We can deal with no elevator.*

My enthusiasm took another blow when we walked into the apartment. The place was dark. Very dark. Our house in Bakersfield had lots of natural light. Not our new home in Frisco. The rooms were dark. The walls were dark. The old shag carpet was dark. However, I tried to look on the bright side and reminded myself that the apartment was roomy, which is what we needed with two boys. The size made up for it being dark and outdated. Lights take care of the dark, so we'd be fine, I said to myself.

My pride did not allow me to admit that all of my research into the perfect place to live in the Dallas area had failed. Instead, I smiled and said something like, "Okay, I'll unload our cars." The look on Kyrah's face told me she was already thinking the same thing I was, that this apartment was not going to work. But the lease was only for three months, I reminded myself. That was one of the reasons I'd picked this apartment complex. A short lease meant that if this move didn't work out the way I'd hoped, we could move back to our paid-off home in Bakersfield and wouldn't have to buy out a long lease. I always like to have a contingency plan, just in case.

The four of us slept on an air mattress in our empty apartment that first night. I got up the next morning and went outside to take a walk. As soon as I opened the door, I knew I wasn't in California anymore. It was freezing, and the wind was so strong I was taken aback. I ran into the apartment and put on sweats and a sweater. I wondered what on earth I was doing in a place like this. When you spend your entire life in a place where your definition of cold is mid-fifties, a thirty-something-degree February day feels like the North Pole. I wasn't prepared for it.

We bundled up the boys and went out to go buy some essentials and drive around to check out the area. When I researched the best places to live in the Dallas area, Frisco was high on the list. That's one of the reasons why I picked it. However, once we started driving around the area, we discovered that we were a long way from Dallas itself. We moved here to be closer to a major city. Frisco didn't feel that close. It was also pretty far from the DFW Airport, which was a big deal because we needed easy access to the airport both for work and to go back and forth to Bakersfield when we needed to get there.

Still, my pride wasn't ready to admit that I could have done a better job at picking out a place to live. However, it was getting harder and harder to deny it. When Kyrah started dragging after a couple more days in our dark apartment, which felt even darker because the sky stayed overcast for days, I knew I had to swallow my pride and get us out of there before our furniture arrived. We loaded the boys back in the car, started driving around, and found another, more central apartment near Irving. Unlike the dark place with shag carpeting, this one had lots of natural light and was only ten minutes from the airport. We signed the lease right then and never spent another night in the dark apartment. Our furniture arrived a week later.

Once we had our furniture, I felt like we could now make the fresh start we'd hoped to make here. We'd find a church and make new friends and settle into life in Dallas. It was still cold. And the sun didn't shine more than it had before, but still, I knew we'd made the right move. We just had to get moving to get this new life started.

That was the first week of March 2020.

On the second week of March 2020, the entire world shut down.

Like everyone else in America, we went into COVID isolation. We couldn't go to church. We couldn't take the boys to the park. We couldn't get out and meet our neighbors. All we could do was sit in our increasingly tiny apartment with two children under two years of age and hope this COVID thing didn't last too long. (As I write this, I'm still wondering how long it will last. Life has yet to return to normal.) Our new normal became sitting in our apartment watching the boys, watching television, trying to work, while every day felt exactly like the day before. I hated it.

By the second or third week of quarantine, I started wondering what we were doing in Dallas. We'd left a paid-off house with a yard, a home gym, warm weather, and family nearby, for what? Back home, life was comfortable. Here…not so much. We'd had absolutely no reason to leave Bakersfield. None. The whole move started to feel like God's comedy. I had never been homesick before in my life, but I was now. I missed my house. I missed my yard. I missed the familiarity of the place I'd lived all my life. And, for the first time in my life, I missed my family. I called my mom one day, and she told me about the whole family getting together for a birthday party. "How can you do that with the quarantine?" I asked.

"We all keep our distance out in the yard," she said.

In the past, I took those kinds of family gatherings for granted. Often I complained on the way over and told Kyrah we weren't going to stay very long. Sometimes we went because our presence was expected, not because we wanted to go. Sitting in our Dallas apartment, watching another episode of *Word Party*, I would have given anything to be back with my family. Just thinking about it made me even more depressed than I already was. I had to find a way out of this.

I started dropping hints to Kyrah that maybe we should admit this was a bad idea and move back home. I complained about the unpredictable winter weather in Texas. I wasn't prepared for the winter cold of February and early March, and I really wasn't prepared for it to be dark and cold and windy and rainy one minute, and then for the sun to come out the next. I added something about how at least we knew it would be hot all the time in Bakersfield. "This isn't what we signed up for" became a regular phrase I used.

Kyrah never bit.

One overcast, cold, rainy day, I grunted something about what a deflating day it was. Kyrah told me she was having a great day. I asked, "How can you not be depressed when the sun is NEVER out?"

"It's not that bad," Kyrah said.

"Not *that* bad?" I said.

She smiled and said, "I don't know what you are complaining about. I like it here."

I could not believe what I was seeing. In the not-too-distant past, Kyrah had struggled with change and I'd had to be the rock she would lean against to get through it. But now, our roles had reversed. She may have had some days she was homesick, but she didn't really show it. I hated it in this new place. I was cold, tired, and depressed. Not Kyrah. If anything, she seemed to be thriving. For me, the apartment felt smaller than it was, and it kept getting smaller every day. *Why are we living here when we have a house?* I kept thinking. *An empty house that still belongs to us!* Keeping our house empty had been part of my overall plan for this move. We'd planned on renting it out until we decided exactly what we were going to do long term. However, I'd told the property management company we'd hired to handle everything for us to contact me BEFORE they agreed to rent the house to anyone. All along, my plan had been that if we got to Texas and hated it, which I did, we could move right back and pick up our old lives where we left off. But the property management company didn't do that. Instead, they contacted me *after* the renters had signed their lease. Now I felt stuck, but I wasn't ready to give up.

Finally, I'd spent one cold, cloudy day too many in quarantine. I said to Kyrah, "This isn't working out like I thought it would. I think this move was meant to teach us a lesson, and I learned it. Maybe it was meant to show us that no matter where we are, we're still the same people. Now that we know that for sure, we can go ahead and go back home."

But then Kyrah said...

KYRAH:

I said, "You moved us out here. Now we are staying."

Kaelin came back with another excuse. "If we stay, our kids will never know who their family is…"

I cut him off. "We knew that was a possibility before we moved, and we still went through with it. I don't want to talk about this again."

I have to admit that I surprised myself as the words came out of my mouth. I knew he was uncomfortable, but I also knew that I had been uncomfortable about the changes that came with getting married. That first year, I had more miserable days than I had ever thought possible. And the same thing had happened right after Karter was born. I'd wanted to sell our house and sell our new cars and move back to our old apartment and our old life. But there was no going back then, just like there was no going back now. We had to keep moving forward. I knew that if I said, "Okay, Kaelin, whatever makes *you* happy," it would only be a matter of time after we moved back to Bakersfield that Kaelin would have that same itch that landed us here. I didn't want to move back and forth, looking for that perfect place. There are no perfect places. Instead of running back home, I knew we both had to just push through. Yes, things looked bad now. Things were bad everywhere, since we were in the middle of a global pandemic. But we had to trust that God did not lead us here by accident. He had a purpose in it, and even though we couldn't see it yet, eventually we would.

Honestly, it felt a little odd to be the one not freaked out by change for once, but it also felt really good. I was able to articulate what I felt without fear of disappointing Kaelin. I wasn't the same girl I had been when we first started dating. No longer was I that girl who didn't know anything about herself or what she wanted in life. I now had a strength and a confidence and a voice I did not have before. It's amazing to see what God will do with a surrendered life.

KAELIN:

No, Kyrah is not the same girl I sat down with and told "I date to marry." She has grown and changed, and I love it. I absolutely love it. We haven't been married that long, but I've already figured out that the beauty of getting married young is that we get to see each other grow and change, and we get to do it together.

When Kyrah told me, "You moved us here. Now we have to stay," I didn't feel threatened. I didn't feel like I had to assert my leadership, like I had to have the final say in everything. She was right, and I was wrong. Thankfully I could see that right away because I'm not the same guy I was many years ago. Back then, I thought I had life all figured out. I thought I had a plan and the means to make that plan come true. God has humbled me in this short time that Kyrah and I have been together, and I know He still has more humbling to do. I still get too sure of myself; I still have days where I think I have it together. Thankfully, God has blessed me with a wife who is patient with me on those days, because she knows I am better than that.

KAELIN AND KYRAH:

Looking back at where our story began, we can't believe how far we've come—from meeting each other outside of a portable classroom in seventh grade to unloading a trailer halfway across the country, from being kids growing up together to raising our own children in marriage. You'd think after being with someone for so long that you'd know them like the back of your hand. And you'd be right…if people didn't change. We have both changed a lot over the years. Some of our best and worst moments have been spent together, yet if we judged each other by those days, it wouldn't share the whole story of our love. Our love is one that is committed to growth. We've learned that our relationship isn't built on the conditions of how well things are going. Instead, our relationship is built on the choice to choose each other every day, no matter how we feel. This commitment has led our life of growing together in love to be a life of many mistakes and even more forgiveness. We can't say we're proud of all the things we've ever done, but we have the grace to have no regrets and the trust to have no secrets. This is the best part of marriage, for even as we struggle with ourselves, unconditional love gives us the confidence to keep moving forward. We haven't exactly been perfect in the way we've carried this out, but we now know the more we forgive, the deeper our love grows.

As we neared the end of writing this book, we began to wonder when the "happily ever after" would come in. After telling the stories of our highs and lows, we were looking to end on a high note when everything would just come together and finally work out. But that never came because that's not real life. Through this journey, we've learned that not only are we not promised a "good life" with no problems, but we're also not as "perfect" for each other as our younger selves thought we were. Of course we love each other and are committed to each other for life, but our growth continues when we accept the fact that we were never created to complete each other. By expecting a perfect relationship, we were setting ourselves up for disappointment. The picture-perfect "happily ever after" is never what it seems. It doesn't exist.

We've made our living appearing to be that coveted "relationship goal" of a couple, but if you've read this far, you know we're just as flawed as anyone else. No matter what you see on the internet or expect in your own relationship, the truth is this: God alone is perfect. And it's only in Him that our "happily ever after" is found.

Our story is one that does not exist without God's hand over it. You've read what could be called divine intervention in how things have come together for us, but what's more important is how things have stayed together in our lives. If it had not been for the hand of the Lord guiding and keeping us in Him, we would have never made it this far. Contrary to what culture has told us, we've learned that we can't possibly be everything we need to be to "complete" each other. In fact, we were never supposed to be. God has joined us together in our union to glorify Him, and when we inevitably fall short of being the perfect partners, we can trust in God to keep us whole.

As we come to the end of this book, we have no idea what the future may hold for us. We're still in the grips of the COVID pandemic, which we hope is over by the time you read these pages. Whether it is or isn't really doesn't matter. We do not know what the future may hold, but we know that whatever God has in store for us, we will face it together. And in the end, that's all the assurance either of us needs.

Acknowledgments

Thank you to everyone who has made this book possible. From our family, friends, and mentors, to our team and supporters. You know who you are, and you know that we love you. We are eternally grateful for your impact on our lives.

About the Authors

Kaelin and **Kyrah Edwards** are YouTube personalities and social media influencers who have impacted millions of people with a brand centered on displaying their faith in the day-to-day journey of life as a young married Christian couple. With millions of followers on social media, they are thought leaders of their generation. Convinced life is not to be lived alone, their audience comes alongside to do life together with them. The couple resides in Dallas, Texas, with their two children, Karter and Kaiser.

Connect with the Edwards family on all major social media platforms @KaelinAndKyrah, or at KaelinAndKyrah.com.